Gastronomical and Culinary Literature:

A Survey and Analysis of
Historically-Oriented Collections
in the U.S.A.

by

BARBARA L. FERET

The Scarecrow Press, Inc.

Metuchen, N.J. & London

1979

This study, conducted in 1975-76, was supported by the Council on Library Resources. The study was revised, 1977-78.

Library of Congress Cataloging in Publication Data

Feret, Barbara L   1940-
    Gastronomical and culinary literature.

    Bibliography: p.
    Includes index.
    1.   Gastronomy--History--Library resources.
2.   Cookery--History--Library resources.   3.   United
States--Library resources.   I.   Title.
Z5776. G2F47   016. 641   78-32098
ISBN 0-8108-1204-5

CONTENTS

iii

PART I

THE LITERATURE

INTRODUCTION

The purpose of this study being to survey, identify, and analyze important U. S. collections of printed materials on the culinary arts, it seems appropriate to first offer some preliminary discussion on the nature and historical development of the literature of cookery and gastronomy before proceeding to the rest.

To those who eat to live, cooking is nothing more than a habit or a daily chore imposed by necessity and reinforced by custom. Humankind must eat and the usual manner of preparing food is common everyday knowledge in all societies. Ways of treating food to make it more palatable have been and continue to be handed down from generation to generation, principally as an oral rather than a written tradition. For this reason, for many cultures there is comparatively little in written form to tell us specifically how food was prepared or served in times past; there is also little to tell us how specific dishes evolved into their present forms.

When there is a certain amount of wealth and leisure, this attitude toward cooking and dining changes. To those who can afford to live to eat, the preparation of food may no longer be an attempt at making a necessity more palatable; rather, cooking may become a delightful amusement or even an absorbing science. Given a sensually receptive and genuinely intellectual attitude, cookery can also develop into what is its best form--an Art. Cookery has been and can be an

3

art whose devoted "artistes" and appreciative "audiences"
may be every bit as avid and enthusiastic as those who ap-
preciate literature, music, architecture, sculpture, dance
and the theatre.

   As Frank Croninshie wrote in his foreword to Brillat-
Savarin's Physiology of Taste (1926): "The sense of taste
falls properly into the realm of esthetics.   A nation that
thinks critically of food is certain to think critically of its
painting, writing, acting, music and objets d'art.   The arts
have always flourished most opulently in cities where people
lived well and paid a reasoned and critical attention to their
senses.   In Athens, Rome, Florence and Paris, art was car-
ried to an unbelievable degree of perfection.   It is significant
that these were the cities also in which entertaining, the social amenities and the arts of dining and banqueting flourished
concurrently....   Painting, architecture and sculpture are
purely visual arts; music is essentially an aural art, the art
of dining involves the mingling of four senses--sight, touch,
taste and smell. "

   There have always been more cooks than writers (or
readers, for that matter), literacy having been the preroga-
tive of only a privileged few until very recently in history.
Many have been the contributors to our Western culinary
repertoire, but relatively few are recorded or known.   The
trade secrets of professional cooks were jealously guarded
and most often conveyed orally only to those who seemed
worthy.   Family recipes and household advice, if written,
were handed down from generation to generation in forms
easily destroyed. · Those creative talents who have actually
published writings in the culinary arts are also few; and the
names of these authors are generally unfamiliar to most people.   Only the occasional gourmet cook or antiquarian biblio-

phile can boast of being acquainted with the writings of Messisbugo, Brillat-Savarin, Galen, Raffald, Beauvilliers and other chefs, physicians, housekeepers, restaurateurs, gourmands and household cooks who have written on the ways and pleasures of cooking and dining.

This unfamiliarity with the names of historically important writers on the culinary arts is not altogether surprising. Recipes and discourses on the relationship of food and drink to health and pleasure are common exchanges in everyday conversation. However much an individual writer or speaker may claim to have come upon something unique, his contribution to the culinary arts is most often a compilation of knowledge orally handed down from times past and, at least in modern times, is usually to be found in many contemporary cookery and household books. If he is a thorough and erudite compounder of popular information, his name becomes familiar to his contemporaries and he is hailed as an "authority." For that reason, most Americans today are familiar with the names of Julia Child, James Beard and even the infamous Betty Crocker, pseud.

Although they are regarded as minor contributions to our cultural heritage, writings on food and physik, cookerye, curtasye and gastronomie have always been popular with the literate. Accounts of feasts, dinners, eating habits, etc. can be found in many of the diaries, biographies, histories and various other essays from the past. Yet there is much lacking. Even though these writings may incidentally chronicle a magnificent dinner or mention a particularly delectable dish or comment on a peculiar food-related custom, they rarely provide detailed information or explain exactly how the food was prepared or served. One is often left with a curt statement: "He was treated to a sumptuous feast"--period.

How the feast was prepared or what the progression of service might have been is left to conjecture.   Writers of this
kind are often concerned with the effect rather than the pro-
cess of cooking and serving.

Manuscript receipts and pre-eighteenth-century books
written specifically to instruct those who served in kitchen
and dining-hall are also surprisingly vague.   Again, much
was handed down orally and it was assumed that a professional cook or housekeeper, given only a fairly general list
of ingredients and a brief notion of processes to be applied,
would know the correct proportions, the proper sequence, the
required processes and finally, how to arrange the ultimate
outcome.   To list foods served in times past is comparatively easy.   To say how the food was cooked or brought to the
table is more difficult.   To trace the historical development
of a particular dish is the most difficult of all.

In addition to being scattered and often vague, printed
materials listed in gastronomic bibliographies can be seen to
be extremely varied in subject, in approach to their subject,
and in the quality of their literary style.   Side by side, one
finds the works of Nicolas Appert, the inventor of the canning process; Claudius Galen, the celebrated authority in
physiology for over 1300 years; John Farley, principal cook
at the London Tavern; Isabel Beeton, housewife; Samuel Peggee, bibliophile; Platina de Cremona, Renaissance scholar.
To determine which of these writings is especially significant
seems to be the task not of a scholar but of a diplomat.
The importance or value of a work is seen very differently
through the eyes of a professional cook or an antiquarian.
The chef will passionately defend Escoffier, Carême, Gouffé
as the only truly important writers.   The housewife will have
little use for "those fancy cooks" and cling to her Fannie

Farmer. The antiquarian will thoughtfully cite the Forme of
Cury. The discriminating sybarite will fondly recall Grimod
de la Reyniere. All of these various audiences and users of
culinary material can legitimately claim to be "authorities"
capable of discussing the significance of a particular work.

For these reasons, the criteria for significance herein
proposed are intended to reflect in some way the expectations
of all of these--the chef, the household cook, the antiquarian,
the gourmand.

First, it would seem that a writer who, in addition
to compounding contemporary information, is able to codify
that information in the light of the past and purposely adjust
it to project a future or a change in the art of cookery,
should be considered a major contributor to culinary literature. This category of significance is reserved for very few.
Here we may place the writings of professional cooks who
have written understandingly on the art--La Varenne, Carême,
Escoffier--all innovators who are recognized as having con-
tributed significantly to the evolutionary development of Western cookery and its documentary literature.

Secondly, when a work reveals a firm grasp of its
subject, so that it becomes very well-known and is referred
to as a useful guiding text for many years, it can be considered a significant contribution to culinary literature. Here
we might place the works of Apicius, Platina, Glasse and
others whose writings went through many editions, some in
several languages.

Thirdly, when a work gives us a rare glimpse of the
customs of the time, it may also be considered an important
piece of culinary literature, even though the authorship be
minor, questionable or even unknown. We might place in
this category the Ménagier de Paris, Roselli's Epulario,

De Verstandighe <u>Kock</u> and others.

      And finally, when an author, in his attempt to describe
the tastes of his time or the tastes of times past, proves to
be especially erudite and provides a compendium of information used as a standard reference source, this work, too,
may be considered important. Here one may list the publications of Brillat-Savarin, Alexandre Dumas and, perhaps,
even the more contemporary André Simon, Prosper Montagné
and Curnonsky.

      These four general criteria for significance in culinary
literature:

1.   recorded major codification and/or innovation in cook-
       ery
2.   many editions or significant popularity
3.   scarcity
4.   standard reference

should not be considered as exclusive. Rather, they are sug-
gested as reasons for the inclusion of titles and library holdings specifically mentioned in this survey. One might suc-
cessfully argue that other works not on cooking or dining
(such as physicians' texts, church society publications, house-
keeping manuals, etiquette books, diaries, philosophical
treatises on esthetics, literary descriptions, histories of
manners and customs, etc.) also provide a significant historical and cultural framework for any conclusions drawn
about the development of the culinary arts. The exclusion of
these types of materials or collections from this study is
not meant to imply that they are unimportant. Rather, it is
an indication of the limited purpose--to consider only the
more significant works and collections in the United States
which are specifically devoted to the culinary arts. With
these criteria in mind, let us proceed to a consideration of
the printed literature.

BEFORE PRINTING

From before the invention of printing there is little written record surviving to tell us about the development of the actual craft of cookery. References to feasts and food items can be found in the writings of ancient philosophers, historians and playwrights and we can ascertain, for instance, that beer was probably first manufactured in Babylonia, or that very few vegetables were eaten in Europe during the Middle Ages, or that ordinary Roman citizens subsisted on readily available fish and barley porridge while the aristocracy feasted on many varieties of meat and game as well as fish. Specific information or directions on how a particular food item was prepared or how its preparation evolved is not at all well detailed or chronicled. There were no recipe books as we know them.

The most pertinent general reference to the cookery of the pre-Christian world is the work of Athenaeus, a Greek scholar of the third century A.D. Called Deipnosophistai (Sophists at Dinner or Connoisseurs in Dining), the fifteen books which comprise this work are presented as a conversation among learned men at a banquet in the year 228 A.D., who are discussing philosophy, literature, music, law and dining. The work actually is a compilation of the writings of past authors.

Another work of a similar nature is De Trinclinio Romano by Petrus Toletanus Ciacconius. This is a compilation

9

of information on the feasts and epulary habits of the
Romans, gathered from ancient authors. It was first
published in Rome in 1588 and went through many editions.

Both the Deipnosophistai and De Trinclinio contain
snatches of information and short quotations from ancient
cookery texts which no longer exist. Only one Latin cookery
text seems to have survived. This work, Apicius' De Re
Culinaria, for the most part, contains lists of ingredients
with no indication of quantities or directions on how they are
to be used. Probably only experienced cooks could have used
the Apicius book, but its simple and direct style and frequent
use of colloquialisms apparently insured its popularity.   It
was copied many times over and seems to have been used as
a basic cookery text from Roman times through the later
Middle Ages, a remarkable span of over a thousand years.

The text that has come down to us is not the original
first-century cookery book of M. Gavius Apicius, but most
probably is the work of an editor who lived in the fourth or
fifth century.   This Apicius--preserved in two ninth-century
manuscripts, excerpts from an eighth-century manuscript,
texts printed during the Renaissance (first edition in 1498)
and subsequent editions and translations--is a compilation
from various sources including Apicius' original recipes, a
Greek cookery book of the Imperial period, a dietetic cookery book, a book on agriculture and domestic science by
Apuleius, medical treatises and several other works (Flower.
The Roman Cookery Book). It was an attempt, and apparently a very successful one, to combine in one book recipes
for the aristocracy and recipes for average middle-class
households in both town and country. "The book's popularity
seems to have risen sharply in the 15th century when 10

manuscripts and 3 printings were made ... that it had a direct influence on medieval cookery is indicated not only by
its rise in popularity in the 15th century, but by the equally
rapid decline at the end of the Middle Ages. After 1542,
there were no new editions until the 18th century" (Norman.
Tales of the Table). As an historical item, it is a melting-
pot of several centuries of cooking and, along with several
other surviving manuscripts, it does give us an early view
of how foods were cooked in the Western world up until the
Renaissance.

        The first completely preserved French cookery book
also gives us a rare view of cookery as practiced in the Middle Ages. Unlike the Apicius compilation of excerpts from
many writers, it is the work of one person who was head
chef of a royal household, an imaginative cook as well as an
orderly compiler. Le Viandier, composed about 1375 A. D.
for the cooks of Charles V of France, was written by Guil-
laume Tirel, called Taillevent, who was chef to Philippe VI
de Valois, Charles V and Charles VI. Recently Paul Ae-
bischer identified a manuscript which he dates before 1320
and which contains the Viandier. He concludes that Taillevent may have written his own version of an already established text. Be that as it may, Taillevent's Le Viandier was
the first attempt to provide an instructive text, giving menus,
directions for preparing particular dishes (especially ragoûts),
recipes for 17 different sauces (using bread as a binder) and
some indication of cooking techniques. This manuscript-
treatise was apparently well known. It was recopied many
times. At least 16 different editions were published, the
first appearing around 1490. In 1461 Francois Villon wrote
in Le Grand Testament: "Si allé veoir en Taillevent/Au cha-
pitre de fricassure. " In 1892, Baron Jerôme Pichon, Presi-

dent of the Société des Bibliophiles François, reprinted the
existing manuscript texts of Le Viandier along with the 16th-
century printed edition, notes, tables of contents, bibliography, etc.

Le Viandier is the oldest French cookbook. The second oldest is the Ménagier de Paris, written about 1392.
Le Livre Fort Excellênt de Cuysine, 1542, is sometimes
described as the oldest French cookery book. Its contents
date from the 14th century and it includes a great number of
the recipes of the Viandier, as they appeared in Le Ménagier.
Le Livre Fort ... was published under several different titles: Le Grand Cuisinier de Toute Cuisine, Le Grand Cuisinier Trés Utille et Proffitable, La Fleur de Toute Cuysine,
Le Livre de Cuysine. A work titled Le Livre de Honneste
Volvpte (Lyon, 1588) is a rearrangement of the Lyon 1555
edition of Le Livre Fort.

Both De Re Coquinaria and Le Viandier are bona fide
cookbooks, originally existing as manuscripts and then appearing early in the history of book printing, apparently by popular demand. There are other significant culinary works
which existed in manuscript form and which were subsequently
printed, but their history is not quite the same. In most
instances, these manuscripts were discovered by an enterpris-
ing printer or a scholarly researcher of a much later date,
who recognized the manuscript as being rare or important
and then published it in a limited edition as an historical
curiosity.

One of the earliest of these was compiled in England,
about 1390 A. D. , as a royal cookbook for the King's household. The Forme of Cury, a vellum roll attributed to the
early 15th century, is probably a compilation dictated by the
cooks of King Richard II. It contains recipes for English-

French dishes developed between the Norman conquest and
the reign of Richard II, a span of three and one-half centuries.   It is the oldest work on cookery in English; the
nomenclature is Norman-French for the most part, with some
names of Saxon derivation.   The manuscript was prepared
"by assent and advisement of masters of physic and philosophy, that dwelled in his [Richard II's] court" (Foreword).
It was printed as a book in 1780 by Dr. Samuel Pegge, a
well-known antiquarian, who presented a full transcript of
the roll with comments, an index, a glossary and an appended
manuscript of the Rolls of Provision of Henry VIII.   Eleven
years later, Richard Warner printed the "Forme of Cury"
in his Antiquitates Culinariae (1791) together with the menus
of several feasts given in the 15th and 16th centuries and
other collections of old receipts, one of which dates from
1381.   As recently as 1975 the New York Metropolitan Museum of Art issued a modernized Christmas gift edition of
The Forme of Cury.

There are other curious manuscripts which were not
written as cookery books but which do closely relate to early
culinary matters:

Alexander Neckham's De Utensilibus or Treatise on Utensils,
    written in Latin and Norman French at the close of
    the 12th century.   Written by the Abbot of Cirencester,
    it describes the furniture and apparatus of a kitchen
    and was intended as a guide to a housekeeper for a
    family of high rank.

Liber Cure Cocorum.   Extant in a 15th-century manuscript,
    this was described as a "metrical treatise ... a rep-
    etition of earlier works" (Hazlitt).   It is thought to
    have been written during the time of Henry VI.   R.
    Morris copied and edited it in 1862 for the London
    Philological Society.

Kalendare de Potages, Leche Metys, Dyuerse Bakemetis.
    This manuscript of recipes dates from about 1430.

It contains numerous bills of fare from banquets and
was printed as a part of Two Fifteenth Century Cookery Books edited by Thomas Austin (1888) along with
other manuscripts from the 1400s, an extensive glossary and index.

The Noble Boke off Cookry.   A manuscript of early recipes,
        dating from 1467, this was first printed in 1500 by
        Richard Pynson, printer to King Henry VIII.   The
        second printing was by John Byddell and the third by
        Robina Napier in 1882.   A Proper New Book of Cook-
        ery (1546) which is often reprinted, is a recension of
        the Boke off Cookry.   The work describes entertain-
        ments from the time of Henry IV to Edward IV and
        gives directions for the cooks of the King's household.
        It is written in the Anglo-French of the period.

John Russell's Boke of Nurture, written about 1450 by the
        "usher and marshal to Humphrey, Duke of Gloucester"
        (foreword) and printed by Frederick J. Furnivall in
        the 1800s.

The Boke of Kervynge.   An early book on carving techniques
        and terms printed by Wynkyn de Worde in 1508 and
        reprinted until 1613.   It is included in Furnivall's
        Early English Meals and Manners, 1868.

Il Libro Della Cucina Del Sec. XIV, listed in the Maggs
        Brothers catalog as a "cookery manuscript of the
        XIVth century first published in Bologna, 1863, in a
        limited edition of 202 copies."

Le Ménagier de Paris.   A manuscript of 1392-94 purportedly
        written by an elderly bourgeois Parisian for his very
        young wife as a guide for a good and useful life after
        his death.   This was first printed under the direction
        of Baron Pichon in 1846.   "It is generally thought that
        the Ménagier was written at the request of Charles
        IV or of Isabella of Bavaria between June 1392 and
        September 1394....   There is nothing to prove that
        the Ménagier is the work of a single author.   In any
        case, certain of the recipes appear to have been di-
        rectly inspired by the Viandier....   As the author or
        authors of the Ménagier, the names of Jehan de Fleury,
        the lawyer Jean Louvenet, the banker Jean La Flamant
        have been suggested" (Guy.   An Illustrated History of
        French Cuisine).

Libro Della Natura et Virtu Della Cose.   A manuscript from
      1440 written by Giovanni Michele Savonarola, famous
      Italian physician, describing types of foods, their prep-
      aration and usefulness in human diet.

ITALY--FIFTEENTH AND SIXTEENTH CENTURIES

The first printed cookery book was not the popular
De Re Coquinaria or Taillevent's Le Viandier or any of the
medieval manuscripts mentioned previously. It was an original work based on a manuscript written by one Maestro Martino, cook to Cardinal Ludovico Trevisan in the early 15th
century. The Martino manuscript, Libro de Arte Coquinaria,
was not the usual disorderly culinary commentary but a sys-
tematic division of 250 recipes into chapters by types of food
(meat, broths and stews, condiments and sauces, pastries,
pies and torten, fried foods and eggs, fish). Two hundred
and forty of these recipes appeared, often in the same order,
in Books VI through X of De Honesta Voluptatae, published
by Bartolomeo Platina in 1475. (There is some question as
to whether the first edition was the dated 1475 Venice edition
or the undated Rome edition.) De Honesta Voluptatae was
the work of a humanist-scholar who, in publishing this text,
was formally announcing that "he had taken the Epicurean
side in the great 15th century literary controversy over
whether the summum bonum is to be attained by the path of
the Stoics, the Peripatetics or the Epicureans" (Beck). This
work, containing the recipes of Maestro Martino, was immediately popular and remained popular for a remarkably pro-
longed period.

By 1541 there were at least 16 Latin editions. An
Italian edition appeared in 1487, a French edition in 1505.

The first Swiss cook book was a 1541 Basel publication of
Apicius and Platina combined in one volume.   The first
Italian cookbook, the Epulario (1516), attributed to one
Giovanni Rosselli, was in reality Martino's recipes with
some additions.   The first Belgian cookbook, Eenen Nyeuwen
Cook Boek, printed in 1560 by Geradus Vorselman, was derived from various sources including 133 of Platina's (Martino's) recipes.   The first Spanish cookbook, Libro de Cozina ... (1520, 1525), attributed to Ruperto de Nola, cook
to one of the Argonese Kings of Naples, was also "permeated
with the Italian culinary culture represented by Platina"
(Beck).

        The rapid distribution of De Honesta Voluptatae can
be seen as a part of the spreading enlightenment of the Renaissance, which increasingly recognized individual competence
and inventiveness.   Martino's manuscript text has been com-
pared with other culinary manuscripts of the period, and
found to be not only more coherent in methodology but also
permeated with "a sensitivity which occasionally goes beyond
simple gustatory and olfactory data to touch upon the plastic
values of culinary practice, on the rapport which exists between foods and utensils used in their preparation, the prep-
arations themselves and the effects they are intended to pro-
duce" (Faccioli).   Platina, the Renaissance humanist and
scholar, thought it worthwhile to include the writings of this
sensitive professional cook in his treatise on the pleasures
of friendship and food and the enjoyment of a blessed life.
The work was very well received and evidently was a major
factor in the development of cookery in Europe.

        For many reasons, including possibly the increasing
communication between skilled chefs and appreciative gastronomes via printed books, the practice of cookery, which had

been almost static for 1300 years, began to change. During the 15th and 16th centuries, the serious French, the esthetic Italians, the exotic Moorish-Spaniards, the German bourgeois encyclopedists began to assert themselves. The move was away from accepted Roman heaviness and disguise to a thoughtful analysis of the natural tastes and textures of foods as well as technical descriptions of what exactly constituted proper preparation and presentation. Although there was much emphasis on French techniques, the main impetus for this evolution in cookery seems to have come from Italy.

A singular landmark in culinary literature published at the time was the Opera of M. Bartolomeo Scappi, "Cuoco Secreto di Papa Pio Quinto." First published at Venice in 1570, the original edition contains almost 900 pages of information about kitchens of the period, the utensils found in them, and hundreds of recipes. There are 27 plates showing the interiors of kitchens and implements used at the time. The book is divided into six parts:

1.   a dialog between the author and his apprentice, Giovanni, on what a head cook should be; a description of a kitchen and the various utensils required by the cook; how to keep particular foods fresh, the wines best suited for making sauces.

2.   two hundred eighty recipes for cooking animals and birds, for sauces, soups, fricassees, mince pies.

3.   two hundred eighteen fish recipes, of which twenty-six refer to sturgeon.

4.   lists of courses for flesh days and days of abstinence; menus for every month in the year, for banquets and for common dinners.

5.   pasta, pies, pastry.

6.   diets for the sick and convalescent, with two hundred recipes.

Principally because of its size and fascinating illustrations, the work is unique for the period. In its later editions, which were published up to the end of the 17th century, two sections were added to this already gigantic compendium:

1. Il Trinciante, written by Vencenzo Cervio, carver to Cardinal Farnese. First published in Venice in 1581, this is a treatise on the duties of the carver and a discussion on the art of carving meat, fish and fruit.

2. Il Mastro di Casa (1581), by Signor Cesare Pandini, Maître d'hôtel to Cardinal Farnese. This is a dialog between a carver and a maître d'hôtel on how to receive nobility and the quality and method of preparing meat, fish, poultry, game, etc. The work seems similar to the Dialogo del Maestro di Casa (1598) of Caesare Evitascandalo, who was Scalo or Maitre d'hôtel to the Imperial Ambassador to the Vatican. It is a four-volume work on Italian cookery, carving and household management, also written as a dialog.

The Banchetti Compositioni di Vivande by Cristoforo di Messisbugo, a native of Moosburg, Bavaria, is also one of the rarest and most beautiful illustrated culinary texts, having been printed in a very elegant manner. First published in Ferrara in 1548 (Messisbugo was seneschal to Don Hippolito d'Este, Cardinal of Ferrara), it was an immediate success and went into several editions up to 1626. Not a singular cookbook, but a record of the household of a Renaissance noble, it begins with a complete inventory of a princely house and reviews memorable banquets and menus, giving their recipes, quantities required, number of servings for each, preparation and the time required for preparation. It is quite unusual to find such explicit directions in a text of this period. Because of its fine detail, this is probably one of the more important Renaissance books on manners and customs, as well as on the foods of the period.

Other important Italian works of the 16th century relating to the culinary arts include:

1. La Singolare Dottrina (1560) by Domenico Romoli, cook
    to Cardinal Farnese. This is a treatise on the art of
    carving meat, the choice, care and serving of wine, the
    nutritive values of various foods and the proper season
    for eating meat and fish as well as directions for cooking.

2. De Re Cibaria (1560) by Joannus Bruyerinus, a twenty-
    two-book treatise on foods and their uses. It has val-
    uable historic information and is quoted frequently in Le
    Grand D'Aussy's Histoire de la Vie Privée des François.

An indication of the popularity of Italian publications
on culinary matters is the distribution of the work of one
Alessio Piemontese (pen name of Giorlamo Ruscelli).   His
Book of Secrets, a collection of recipes and remedies, was
first published in Italian (Venice, 1555), then French (Antwerp, 1557), then English (London, 1558), Latin (Basle,
1559), Dutch (Antwerp, 1561) and German (Basle, 1575).

The interweaving of French and Italian influence in the
evolution of Western cookery is confusing to the researcher
determined to choose one over the other.   During the latter
middle ages and early Renaissance, the French kings fought
a series of wars with Italy and there was a good deal of
diplomatic intermingling.   Catherine de Medici, whose com-
ing to France in 1533 is often marked as a culinary turning
point, was the daughter of Lorenzo II de Medici and a French
princess, Madelaine de la Tour d'Auvergne.   Her arrival was
preceded by the translation of Platina into French and by the
general availability of Taillevent's Viandier.   It seems that up
to the middle of the 17th century, Popes, Kings and the lesser
nobility favored Italian culinary artisans, but with the shifting of
the cultural centers of Europe from Florence, Venice and Rome
to Versailles, French influence began to dominate the culinary
field.

FRANCE AND ITALY--SEVENTEENTH CENTURY

The cuisine which began evolving during the Renaissance
was lighter than that of the Middle Ages, but still dominated
by the heavy use of sugar and spices and a mixing of savories
and sweets throughout the service of a meal. It was in the
mid-seventeenth century that a French work appeared which
announced that a major turning point had been reached in the
development of fine cuisine--Le Cuisinier François (Paris,
1651) by Pierre François de la Varenne. Monsieur La
Varenne purportedly began his career as kitchen minion in
the home of the Dutchess de Bar, sister of Henry IV of
France, and may have served in the kitchens of Marie de
Medici, a cousin of Catherine, who married Henry IV of
France in 1600. His recipes, the first ever to be presented
in alphabetical order, indicate that cooking had changed. The
heavily used spices of the Middle Ages were discarded and
replaced with delicate seasonings and meat and vegetable es-
sences. Roasts were to be served in their natural juices
or finished off with simple sauces based on meat drippings.
A roux of flour and fat replaced Taillevent's coarse bread
crumbs for thickening. Entrements were used to divorce
savories from sweets. Butter was used instead of oil or
meat fat in pastries. Recipes were given for puff paste,
petits fours. There were over sixty recipes for the preparation of eggs. Basic bouillon, bouquet garni, cream soup,
the haute cuisine duxelles sauce of mushrooms and onions

appeared (La Varenne called it Champignons à la Olivier),
and directions were given for preparing vegetables. The
cuisine detailed by La Varenne was more delicate and apparently more appealing than what had come before. Le Cuisinier François immediately became popular, going into many
French editions. Vicaire writes: "Brunet indique au Manuel
un Confiturier François du Sieur La Varenne, publié à Paris
en 1650." Vicaire believed that Le Pastissier François
(1653) was written by La Varenne. The latter was often published in conjunction with Le Cuisinier François. Very
shortly after it appeared in Paris (1651) Le Cuisinier François was translated into English (London, 1654). Le Pastissier François (1653) also appeared in English very quickly as
the first part of Marmette's The Perfect Cook (1656). An
Italian edition of Le Cuisinier François appeared at Bologna
in 1690. "Food was no longer to be disguised, but appre-
ciated for its true flavor. The object of cooking ... was to
bring out the natural flavor of a food, not hide it, a key point
of modern French cooking" (Claiborne. Classic French Cooking).

Notwithstanding the call for naturalness, an astonish-
ingly varied profusion of dishes was served in France during
the 17th century. Many are described by Nicholas de Bonnefons, the Valet de Chambre du Roi, in his Les Délices de
la Campagne (1654). This work is divided into three parts:
1) bread, cakes, wine and beverages in general; 2) vegetables,
fruits, eggs, milk and cheese; 3) poultry, meat and fish.
It is a companion volume to Le Jardinier François (1651),
which is also divided into three parts: 1) fruit trees and
varieties of fruit that could be grown around Paris; 2) fruits
and vegetables; 3) methods of preserving fruits, making preserves, marzipan and macaroons.

The most encyclopedic of French works published at
the time was L'Escole Parfaite des Officiers de Bouche (Paris,
1662).   It first appeared as a work divided into six sections.
The sections were often reissued as separate books as well
as in a single volume:

> Le Vray Maistre d'Hostel
> Le Grand Escuyer-Tranchant
> Le Sommelier Royal
> Le Confiturier Royal
> Le Cuisinier Royal
> Le Pastissier Royal.

In this work recipes are given for preparing meat, vegetables,
fruit dishes, confectionary.   Kitchen equipment is detailed
and table arrangements explained.   Diagrams show the manner of carving meat and fowl, and how to cut fruit into or-
namental shapes.   The work in its entirety was translated
into English by Giles Rose in 1682 as School of Instruction
for the Officers of the Mouth.   The French edition remained
popular and was published up until 1742.

During the 17th century there was a great deal of interweaving of the French and the Italian approaches to the culinary arts.   Finesse in cookery was increasingly being considered a French talent, while the art of serving and grace-
fully managing a household continued to be associated with
the Italians.   The most influential work on carving published
during the 17th century was a 1639 Italian publication variously
referred to as:

> Il Trinciante di Messer Mattia Giegher Bauaro di Mos-
> burc
> Lo Scalo di M. Mattia Giegher Bauaro di Mosburc
> Li Tre Trattati di Messer Mattia Giegher Bavaro di
> Mosburc.

Lord Westbury states that this was "The most important
work on carving and its ancillaries to have been produced in

the XVII century. Almost all other works to appear on the
subject in various languages were for the most part, slavish
copies of it.... Giegher was purportedly the Bavarian chef
to the University of Padova. The work has 48 plates and a
portrait including engravings on the art of napkin folding,
with over 70 examples. The plates from the Tre Tratati
appear in L'Escole Parfaite des Officiers de Bouche (1662),
in Pierre Petit's L'Art de Trancher la Viande (1647), in
Jacques Vontet's La Vraye Mettode de Bien Trencher (1647)
and in other works of a similar nature."

Other titles of note published in Italy and France during the 17th century include:

Ottaviano Rabasco's Il Convito (1615), a handbook on banquets.

Vittorio Lancelloti of Camerino's Lo Scalo Prattico (1627),
      which gives the menus of a number of banquets served
      in the palace of Cardinal Ippolito Aldobrandino.

Antonio Frugoli's Pratica Escalaria (1632), which is composed
      of seven books on culinary life including: 1) Banquets
      of the Italians, Spanish, French and Germans; 2) Qual-
      ity of foods; 3) Fish and d'eau douce; 4) Condiments
      and legumes; 5) Herbs; 6) Drinks; 7) Antique and mod-
      ern food and drink.

The Archidipno Overo dell-Insalata of Salvatore Massonio
      (1627), a unique book on salads with 68 chapters de-
      voted to different salad dressings and a discussion on
      the types of salads eaten in antiquity. (John Evelyn's
      Acetaria; A Discourse of Sallets, London, 1699, is
      the earliest English work upon salads.)

Le Nouveau Cuisinier (1656) of Pierre De Lune, the Escuyer
      de Cuisine of the Duc de Rohan and the Dutchess d'Or-
      léans, composed as an instructional text for apprentice
      cooks.

Audiger's La Maison Reglée (1692), which includes, along
      with advice for the management of noble households,
      information on wages and the living conditions of people
      of lesser means.

Massialot's <u>Le Cuisinier Roïal et Bourgeois</u> (1691), in two
 parts: 1) Instruction on how to serve meals; 2) Dictionary of dishes in alphabetical order. This was
 very popular and went through many editions.

ITALY--EIGHTEENTH TO TWENTIETH CENTURY

From the middle of the 17th century, French influence
dominated Italian cookery.   Many publications issued in Italy
were simply translations from the French.   La Varenne's
work was translated into Italian in 1680 and was still being
reprinted as late as 1815.   It was not until the mid-18th
century that Italy began to move back to native culinary tra-
ditions.   Following the 1773 issuing in Naples of Vincenzo
Corrado's treatise on sugar, hot beverages and sherbet, Il
Cuoco Galante, a series of Italian cookery texts began to appear.   The best known of these are Nebbia's Cuoco Macera-
tese (1780), the anonymous Il Cuoco Piemontese (1766) and
Francesco Leonardi's encyclopedic L'Apicio Moderno (1790),
written by a man who was once chef to Catherine the Great
of Russia.   Although based on French techniques and descriptive of dishes from many countries, Leonardi's work is emphatically Italian.   Foreign recipes are "adapted" using Italian
ingredients.   The use of the tomato in southern Italian cuisine
is recorded.   After L'Apicio Moderno only two other works
of real note appeared in Italy--La Cucina Teorico-pratica
(1841) by Don Ippolito Cavalcanti, a Neapolitan nobleman,
and the classic La Scienza in Cucina (1880) by Pellegrino
Artusi.

26

GERMANY

The expert cookery and household management texts published in Italy and France during the sixteenth and seventeenth centuries were produced only in limited numbers and were intended for the use of the princely class. In Germany, cookbooks had a wider scope, appealing to the growing middle class--the Hausfrau as well as the court cook. After a rather slow beginning, Germany became a prolific producer of cookery texts aimed at various kinds of audiences.

The first printed German-language cookbook appeared anonymously in Nürnberg in 1485, titled simply Küchenmaysterey. It contains five parts: fast-day foods, meats, baked and fried foods, sauces, wine, and is perhaps the rarest of German culinary publications. The oldest Czech cookery book, Kucharzstwy o Rozlichuch Krmh (1570?), is derived from the German Küchenmeisterei.) The most often mentioned German work of the sixteenth century is Ein Neu Kochbuch (Nürnberg, 1531) by Master Chef Marx von Rumpolt, cook to the Elector of Mainz and to the Queen of Denmark. This huge tome, charmingly illustrated with woodblocks of animals, fish, etc., lists recipes for beef, veal, mutton, salads, vegetables and other dishes.

An early Swiss cookery book, Ars Magirica (1556), written by Willichius, professor of Greek and Medicine at Frankfort, gives information not only on cookery but also on utensils, gourmands, food, etc. A comparative work is

Giocamo Procacchi's Trincier oder Vorleg-Buch (1624, Leipsig), which discusses food as the Italians and Romans prepared it.   George Philipp Haarsdorffer, in the foreword to
his Vollständiges und von Neuen Vermehrtes Trincir-Buch
(1665) acknowledges his debt to Giocomo Procacchi of Ancona
as well as to Matthias Giegher of Mosburg in Bavaria.   This
book has many copper plates of knives and forks, how to fold
napkins, carve fruits, etc. , and is considered one of the
most interesting of illustrated books on table manners.

Two publications illustrating slightly different approaches appeared toward the end of the 16th century:

At Frankfort, in 1564, Gaultherus Ryff, Physician of
Strasburg, published his treatise on dietetics and cookery,
including cookery for the sick.   This New Kochbuch subsequently became known as the authoritative work on dietetics.

At Basle in Switzerland, Anna Wecker, the wife of
the physician Wecker, published a cookery book with recipes
for the sick, for pregnant women, and for the aged.   Titled
Ein Köstlich Neu Kochbuch von Allerhand Speisen (Altorff,
1596), it became the popular authority on dietetics.   It was
frequently reprinted and was issued in Danish in 1648.

Other early and unusual German language works include:

Ramigen's Von den Aromaten (1580), one of the earliest treatises on spices.

Balthaser Staindl von Dillingen's Ein Künstlichs und
Nutzliches Kochbuch (Augsburg, 1564).

Aegidius Albertinus' Zwey Schöne Tractätl--two works
in one volume which contains minute descriptions
of banquets, social life, morals, eating and drinking customs in Germany as well as Antonio de
Guevara's detailed critique of Spanish court life.
(The Spanish original seems to be lost.)

Arnald of Villanova's treatise on wine, printed in
Germany by Wilhelm van Hirnkofen, 1478.

Weltliche Grosse und Gering Haushaltungen, published
at Molsheim in southern Germany in 1671. This
is a cook book for small religious as well as lay
establishments.

De Verstandighe Koch of Sorghvuldighe Huys Houdster,
published in Dutch in Brussels (1672).

An especially intriguing book is Ein Guot Lere von
Guoter Spise, published in the Swabian dialect by Maurer
Constant in Stuttgart in 1844 but said to date back to the 14th
century.

Beginning at the end of the 17th century, it apparently
became fashionable in Germany to publish cookbooks repre-
sentative of the talents of the cooks of particular towns. The
Nurnberger Kochbuch (1691), the Braunschweiger Kochbuch
(1697) and the Leipziger Kochbuch (1712) appeared at that
time. A Kuch und Keller Dictionarin by Pawl Jacob Masperger
appeared in Hamburg in 1716. From the beginning of the 18th
century there was a proliferation of cookbooks in the German
language.

One of the more interesting of the more recent works
is the Ober Heinishches Koch (Mülhausen: Fisseler, 3rd. ed.
1819-1820, 2 volumes), which deals with the gastronomy of
Alsace. Written by a protestant minister's wife, Mrs. Spoer-
lin, this book was probably the inspiration for the well-known
work of Charles Gérard, L'Ancienne Alsace à Table (1862),
written in French, published in Germany--an excellent volume
on the food and manners of the ancient province of Alsace.

SPAIN

In terms of culinary history and bibliography, Spain is an anomaly. The development of Spanish cookery was different from that of the rest of Europe, since Spain was under Moorish influence for almost eight hundred years. The courts of the Sevillian kings during the Middle Ages were distinguished by a luxury that contrasted vividly with the simplicity and coarseness of their contemporary Christian monarchs. The culinary disposition of these Moslem sovereigns is known through the writings of teachers and physicians to the court. Between the 9th and 12th centuries, Ziryab of Baghdad introduced the recipes of the Orient to Spain and established rules to be followed in serving a sumptuous meal. In the middle of the 14th century the Marques de Villena wrote Arte Cisoria (Art of Carving), which was printed in 1766 in Madrid.

Spanish cuisine bears little resemblance to that of Italy, even though the same Mediterranean foods are used. Spices from the Orient--cinnamon, cumin, aniseed, saffron, cloves--are used extensively, as well as rice. Very little pasta is used. Fruits appear in meat or rice dishes as they do in Persia. Spanish pastries are like those of the Near East.

Beginning in the 18th century, Moorish Spain began to be influenced by the French courts and by the New World. The tomato, pepper and potato began to appear in Spanish

cookery. It was only during the time of Charles V and
Philip II that a few cook books were published. Astonishing-
ly, these reveal a strong French bias. It is believed that
many Spanish dishes were adopted by the French and are now
generally considered as a part of classic French cuisine.
The Duc de Richelieu, for example, is credited with importing
to France a sauce called mahonesa, which was presumably
mayonnaise from Mahon in the Balearic Islands. The wives
of three French sovereigns were Spanish: Anne of Austria,
Infanta of Spain, wife of Louis XII, who introduced Spanish
pastries and Sauce Espagnolé; Maria Theresa, Spanish Infanta,
wife of Louis XIV, who abhorred French dishes and brought
with her a Spanish cook named La Molina; Eugenia de Monti-
jo, wife of Napoleon III, who is mentioned in connection with
recipes entitled à l'Eugénie and à l'impératrice. When Napoleon I's troops sacked the library of the Monastery of Alcántara
on the way to Portugal in 1807, the friars' recipe book was
saved and came into the hands of the wife of General Junot,
whose chef, the famous Carême, introduced a number of the
friars' dishes to France (Norman. Spanish Cookbook).

In Barcelona in 1477, the Libre de Coch appeared,
written in Catalan by Maestre Rupert. For more than a
century it was reedited and reprinted many times. In Toledo,
in 1525, it appeared in the Castilian dialect as Libro de
Cozina by Roberto de Nola, cook to King Ferdinand of Naples.
In 1529 it appeared as Libro de Guisados (Book of Stews).
The work may actually be Italian, rather than Spanish in origin.

In 1610 the Art de Cocina appeared, written by Francisco Martínez Montiño, chief cook to King Philippe III of
Spain. It too was reissued many times, the latest edition
appearing in Madrid in 1800.

Three other rare Spanish culinary texts are:

Domingo Hernandez de Maceras' Libro del Arte de Cozina
(1607).

Juan Altamiras' Nuevo Arte de Cocina (Madrid, 1756), with
recipes for meat, fish, vegetables, snails, frogs.

Juan de la Mata's Arte de Reposteria en que se Contiene
Todo (Madrid, 1755), written by the butler to the King
of Spain. With the exception of a chapter on gaspachos,
it is pirated from Massialot's Nouvelle Instruction (the
1716 edition).

ENGLAND--SEVENTEENTH CENTURY

As in Germany, the publication of culinary literature
in England began slowly but grew to larger proportions. The
first printed English cookery book came off the Caxton press
in 1500. It was emphatically titled This Is the Boke of
Cokery "intended for a Princys Household or Any Other Es-
tates." In 1539 the Castel of Helth appeared and in 1585
came The Good Huswifes Jewell which offered "most excellent
and rare divises for conceites in Cookery, found out by the
practise of Thomas Dawson."

More cookery books were produced in England than in
any other Western country during the seventeenth century.
The year 1609 saw the publication of Delightes for Ladies by
Sir Hugh Plat, and in 1615 the most influential of early En-
glish cookery-related texts appeared, The English House-wife
of Gervase Markham. This was probably the most popular
English household book up until about 1683. John Murrel's
Two Bookes of Cookerie and Carving, "according to the new
English and French fashion," was issued during the 1630s.
In 1656 a three-part cookery-medical book appeared: Part
One, The Queen's Closet Opened, gave medical advice and
receipts; Part Two, A Queen's Delight or the Art of Preserving; Part Three, The Compleat Cook, Expertly Prescrib-
ing the Most Ready Ways, Whether Italian, Spanish, or
French, for Dressing of Flesh and Fish, Ordering of Sauces
or Making of Pastry. The recipes were purportedly those

33

of Queen Henrietta Maria, the French wife of Charles I.
William Rabisha also published a three-part work in 1661,
titled The Whole Body of Cookery Dissected.

English cookery books were written by persons from
various walks of life.   In 1660, Robert May, who was the
son of a cook and apprenticed in France, wrote The Accomplisht Cook.   This work contains interesting bills of fare,
well-representative of the era, including a thorough description of a Christmas feast.   In 1669, the work of a Knight,
The Closet of the Eminently Learned Sir Kenelme Digby, was
printed posthumously by permission of his son, John.   Much
of the knight's treatise is about alcoholic beverages.   There
are over 100 recipes for mead.   In 1670, Hannah Woolley,
a lady who enjoyed letter writing, published The Queen-Like
Closet, with recipes, menus and directions to servants.

ENGLAND AND FRANCE--EIGHTEENTH CENTURY

As printed materials became more common, the writers of books on culinary matters and the audiences for these books grew, especially in England and in France. Innkeepers and housewives, as well as professional cooks and chefs of noble households, eagerly devoured the newly issued publications. French taste was dominant, but English practicality had its equal say. The most often mentioned works of the time are:

1709   The Queen's Royal Cookery of T. Hall, who was a "Free Cook of London" and apparently often engaged to cook in the kitchens of Queen Anne, a noted gourmand.

1710   Royal Cookery by Patrick Lamb, Master-Cook at St. James Palace, Hampton Court and Windsor for nearly fifty years, serving Queen Anne, Charles II, James II, and William and Mary. His work includes some Dutch methods. It was published shortly after his death.

1714   A Collection of Above 300 Receipts by Mary Kettilby.

1714   Louis Liger's Dictionnaire Pratique du Bon Menager de Campagne et de Ville--said to be a compilation and rearrangement of the two works of Nicolas de Bonnefons. La Nouvelle Maison Rustique, which was published anonymously, is also attributed to Liger.

1723   John Nott's Cooks and Confectioners Dictionary, which was addressed to the English housewife but evidences much French material. Nott was the Cook to the Duke of Bolton.

1730   Kidder's Receipts of Pastry and Cookery, for the schol-
        ars of his school of cookery.

1730   The Complete Practical Cook by Thomas Carter, cook
        to Lord Cornwallis.

1733   The Modern Cook by Vincent La Chapelle, Chef de
        Cuisine to the Prince of Orange and the Earl of Ches-
        terfield.   La Chapelle was a Frenchman who lived in
        England.   His work was first published in English and
        then translated into French in 1735.   It is one of the
        most reliable of reference books on cookery and dining
        during the 18th century.

1739   The work of Marin, chef to Madame Gesvres and then
        Maître d'Hôtel to the Duc de Soubise: Le Dons de
        Comus (1739), which is divided into three parts: Part
        1 has 12 chapters on potages and the preparation of
        foods; Part 2 has 6 chapters on hors d'oeuvres, entre-
        ments and sauces; Part 3 has menus for the four sea-
        sons.   A preface written by two Jesuits, giving an
        interesting history of the art of the cook, appears in
        all but the first edition of this work.

1739   The writings of Menon: La Cuisinière Bourgeoise (1746),
        which was the most often reprinted French culinary
        book during the latter half of the 18th century; Le
        Soupers de la Cour (1755), the most celebrated of his
        works, which describes banquets and the haute cuisine
        of the royal household; Le Nouveau Traité de la Cui-
        sine (1739); La Nouvelle Cuisine (1742).

1747   The Art of Cookery Made Plain and Easy by a Lady,
        later identified as Hannah Glasse.   This was the best
        seller in cookbooks for over one hundred years.

1751   Le Cannamélliste Français by Joseph Gilliers, Chef
        d'Office to the King of Poland.   This is considered one
        of the finest books on confectionery, candy making and
        pastry decoration.   It is esteemed by artists and jew-
        elers because of its fine etchings illustrating tableware.

1759   William Verral's A Complete System of Cookery.   The
        dishes mentioned are given in both French and English.

1769   The Experienced English Housekeeper by Elizabeth Raf-
        fald, Housekeeper to Lady Worburton, keeper of a con-
        fectioner's shop and three different inns in succession.

The work has over 800 recipes and apparently was
very popular, going through many editions until 1825.

1772   Susannah Carter's The Frugal Housewife, which appeared
in America as a reprint of a London edition, undated,
with plates by Paul Revere.

1782   Le Grand D'Aussy, Pierre Jean Baptiste, Histoire de
la Vie Privée. The finest work on the social life of
the French. It is much valued for its historical references on foods and cookery.

1783   The London Art of Cookery, written by John Farley,
who ran the very successful London Tavern, famous
for its large banquets.

1788   The New Art of Cookery by Richard Briggs, cook at
several taverns in London. This was reprinted in the
United States and remained unequalled in size or con-
tent by any other American cookbook until the middle
of the 19th century.

1789   Frederick Nutt's The Complete Confectioner and The
Imperial and Royal Cook.

ENGLAND AND FRANCE--NINETEENTH
AND TWENTIETH CENTURIES

The 19th century witnessed increasing use of the stove rather than the fireplace for cooking. It also saw the triumph of French culinary artistry throughout most of the Western World. Although many works written for the English housewife appeared, the French chefs and French writers on culinary matters were looked to for inspiration and authority.

In 1802, the first restaurant reviews began to appear, written by Alexandre Laurent-Balthazar Grimod de la Reynière. Between 1803 and 1812 he issued eight volumes of the Almanach des Gourmands, a critical review of Parisian culinary establishments. In 1808 Grimod de la Reynière wrote the Manuel des Amphitryons, dealing with the art of carving, bills of fare for each season, and table proprieties. Unlike previous "Ecuyer Tranchant" titles, which were written for noble houses, this work was intended to introduce the new upper classes to the niceties of an elegant table.

The cause of culinary appreciation was further advanced by Jean Anthelme Brillat-Savarin, a lawyer, who at the age of seventy published one of the most witty discussions on food ever written, Physiologie du Goût (1825). The work is filled with entertaining anecdotes and commentary on good eating, including several pages of impressions about the United States, which he visited from 1794 to 1797. It continues to be published to this day.

Followers in Brillat-Savarin's footsteps include:

Léon il de Fonse Brisse (Baron Brisse), a journalist who specialized in articles on gastronomy written for house-wives. In 1860 he began writing the first daily column on cookery in the newspaper La Liberté. Menus and recipes from this column were later gathered into a publication Le Calendrier Gastronomique; Les 365 Menus du l'Anneé 1867.

Pierre Charles Monselet, a French litterateur who published sonnets and prose related to gastronomy in his L'Almanach Gourmand, issued every year for five years (1886-1870).

Thomas Walker, an English lawyer who wrote a series of essays on The Art of Dining (1835).

The changes which were occurring in the nature of governance during the 19th century are especially well-re-flected in the changing titles of a work written by A. Viard in 1802. It first appeared as Le Cuisinier Impérial and went through 32 editions with a variety of titles: Le Cuisinier Royal, Le Cuisinier National, etc.

At the beginning of the 19th century A New System of Domestic Cookery (1808) was published anonymously "By a Lady," later identified as Mrs. Rundell. By 1846 it had reached 69 editions in London. The work was also very popular in America, where it was first issued under the original title in 1807 and as The Experienced American House-keeper from 1823 onwards.

A revolutionary treatise written by a Parisian confec-tioner and manufacturer of cordials appeared in 1811. Titled L'Art de Conserver by Appert, it explained the canning pro-cess. It was immediately translated into German and English. "What to do" in cookery was beginning to be augmented by "Why it is done."

A name well-known at the time was that of Beauvilliers; but, it referred to two persons. M. Beauvilliers (or
Bauvilliers) apparently was a Maître d'Hôtel who published a
Manuel de la Cuisine in Mentz in 1811. This work subsequently appeared as Le Nouveau Cuisinier Royal (Paris,
1835) and as Le Bon et Parfait Cuisinier Universel (Paris,
1837). Antoine Beauvilliers, on the other hand, was a famous Parisian restaurateur who, in 1782, opened one of the
first true restaurants, the Grand Taverne de Londres. His
L'Art du Cuisinier (Paris, 1814), though primarily French, did
claim to include "the best of English cookery which I have
had the advantage of being the first to transplant to France."
It appeared as The Art of French Cookery in London in 1824.
At the time of publication it was considered to be the most
reliable and best treatise on cooking available.

Another well-known name was Louis Eustache Ude,
once chef to Louis XVI, Maître d'Hôtel to Madame Letetia
Bonaparte, the mother of Napoleon, and later steward and
manager of the St. James Club in London. It was Ude who
introduced the light sandwich supper at fashionable soirées.
His French Cook appeared in 1813 and had run into 14 editions by 1841.

It is, however, M. Antonin Carême (1783-1833) who
emerges as the most famous culinary figure of the 19th century. Chef to Talleyrand, Czar Alexander, Louis XVIII, the
Baron de Rothschild and other important personages, he was
both a model and a symbol for many cooks, especially in
England. Carême wrote and published several books at his
own expense and later sold the rights to publishers Fayot.
Though his recipes are far too elaborate for modern domestic
use, they do provide the first really detailed description of
French Haute Cuisine. Titles include:

Le Patissier Royal, 1815.
L'Art de la Cuisine Française, three volumes, 1833
    (Three more volumes were added later by Plumé-
    rey.)
Le Cuisinier Parisien, 1828.
Le Patissier Pittoresque, 1815.
Le Maître d'Hôtel Français, 1822.

To women, the most important culinary figure of the
19th century was not Carême but Isabella Beeton, a housewife who died at the young age of 28.   Her Book of Household Management, first serialized in the Englishwoman's Domestic Magazine (1859-1861) and then published as a book in
1860, became the culinary best seller of the Victorian era.
It is still published today in various abbreviated forms.

The French Betty Crocker of the 19th century seems
to have been Louis Eustache Audot, who wrote La Cuisinière de la
Campagne et de la Ville in 1818, translated and adapted as
French Domestic Cookery in 1846.

The 19th century is replete with the names of famous
chefs and their writings:

Etienne, whose Traité de l'Office, is considered to be
one of the most complete works on table service, hors
d'oeuvres, salads, desserts, ices.   It appeared as
part of the Carême collection and then was published
as a separate volume in 1845.

Alexis Soyer, versatile chef, who ran a luxury restaurant, a soup kitchen, invented a military cooking
stove and managed to write nine works on cookery
ranging from The Pantropheon or History of Food (1853)
to A Shilling Cookery for the People (1845).

Charles Elmé Francatelli, pupil of Carême, chef to
Queen Victoria, who wrote The Modern Cook (1853)
and The Royal Confectioner (1862).

Jules Gouffé, also a pupil of Carême, whose books
were written for chefs who had high professional skills
and were able to afford great expenditures: Le Livre

de Cuisine (1867) or Royal Cookery Book (1869); Le
Livre de Patisserie (1873); Le Livre des Soupes et
des Potages (1875); Le Livre des Conserves (1869) or
Book of Preserves (1871).   His brother, Alphonse,
who was pastry chef to Queen Victoria, translated his
works into English.

Urbain Dubois, chef to the King and Queen of Prussia,
who wrote six important works on cookery.   He is
credited with introducing the custom of having servants
wait table or service à lá Russe.

Surprisingly, the name of Alexandre Dumas also ap-
pears in culinary bibliographies because of his last work,
the Grand Dictionnaire de Cuisine (1873).   Written by an am-
ateur, it presents French and foreign classical recipes in a
manner more suited to the non-professional cook.

The 20th century brings us to a person who has been
called the "King of Chefs and Chef of Kings"--August Escoffier.   After working at a number of hotels in France, Escoffier became Chef-des-Cuisines at the Savoy Hotel and Carlton
Hotel.   It has been said that "Escoffier forged a new concept,
replacing Gargantuan plenitude and baroque splendor with
classic simplicity....   He lacked the wit of Brillat-Savarin,
but Brillat-Savarin was more gourmet than cook.   He lacked
the temperament of the great 17th century chef, Vatel, but
was more imaginative" (Le Guide Culinaire, 1903).   Escoffier's Guide to Modern Cookery, published in 1907, is an
exposition and analysis of cookery that has become a "Bible"
for the professional chefs of today.

Other fairly recent French and English writers whose
names seem destined to be considered as important in culinary literature include:

Henri Babinski, better known under his pseudonym
Ali-Bab, author of the huge Gastronomique Pratique
on classic and regional French cookery.   The work

was recently translated into English as <u>The Encyclope-dia of Practical Gastronomy</u> (1974).

Maurice Edmond Sailland, better known under his pseudonym Curnonsky or as the Prince of Gastronomes. He wrote many detailed guides to the gastronomic regions of France. An abridged version of one of his collected works was translated into English as <u>Traditional Recipes of the Provinces of France</u> (1961).

André Simon, founder of the International Wine and Food Society, prolific writer on foods, wines and the art of dining.

Prosper Montagné, noted chef and contemporary of Escoffier. He is best known as the author of <u>La Grande Cuisine Illustrée</u>, in collaboration with Prosper Salles, and of the encyclopedic <u>Larousse Gastronomique</u>.

Fernand Point, patron-chef of the celebrated Pyramide restaurant in Vienne, France. In 1969, a work titled <u>Ma Gastronomie</u> was published containing a few of his recipes and descriptive-biographical material. The work was translated into English in 1974.

UNITED STATES--EIGHTEENTH, NINETEENTH
AND TWENTIETH CENTURIES

Being a fairly recently formed country, the United
States of America has a shorter history of culinary publication than those mentioned previously. Early colonists brought
with them handwritten manuscripts or imported works principally from England. Two of the more popular items were
Hannah Glasse's Art of Cookery and the Complete Housewife
by Mrs. Eliza Smith, the latter having the distinction of
being the first of many American reprints of English cookbooks. Originally published in England in 1727, it was reprinted in 1742 by William Parks, Williamsburg, Virginia.

The first truly American cookbook was American
Cookery by Amelia Simmons (Hartford, Connecticut, 1796).
Although some of the recipes are borrowed from British
cookbooks, notably Susannah Carter's Frugal Housewife, the
work contains the first printed recipes for such American
specialities as Indian pudding, pumpkin pie, Johnny cake,
pickled watermelon rind, soft gingerbread, and Jerusalem
artichokes. It also recommended the use of a chemical
leaven, pearlash, in dough, which process later developed
into the compounding of baking powder. There is no doubt
that it was the foremost cookbook published in the United
States until 1829. It went through a number of editions and
many plagiarized versions. British publishers began placing
in their new editions of older cookbooks recipes taken from

American cookery (clams, pumpkin pie, spruce beer, etc.).

In contrast to American Cookery, which evidenced strong British origins, the second American cookbook of importance revealed the influence of the French culinary heritage as well as that of other countries. The Virginia House-Wife by Mrs. Mary Randolph, published in 1824, may be called the first southern cookbook. Whereas Amelia Simmons mentions specialities of New England, Mary Randolph put in print for the first time dishes typical of the South--catfish soup, turnip tops, beaten biscuits, field peas and ochra soup, along with omelettes, ice cream, doughnuts, Naples biscuits, polenta, curry and Indian meal pudding.

When American Cookery was printed in 1796, presses were small and printers served a limited market. Between 1830 and 1860 the publishing field in the U.S. became an extensive business and more books on household management and cookery began to appear. The four major authors of such books at this time were: Mrs. Lydia Child, Miss Eliza Leslie, Miss Catharine Beecher, Mrs. Sarah Hale. All were prolific writers, not only of cookbooks, but of many other types of works. Eliza Leslie and Lydia Child organized and simplified the culinary knowledge of housewives of their day. They were not pioneers like Amelia Simmons and Mary Randolph. Their books are compendiums of recipes from all parts of the U.S.--such as Moravian sugar-cake, New York cookies, Italian creams, Tennessee muffins, Carolina grits, Yankee chowder, Irish stew, chicken gumbo, etc. Catherine Beecher's works were concerned with "domestic economy as a branch of study" and are considered today as the foundation of home economics in the U.S. Sarah Hale, as the editor of the popular magazine Godey's Lady's Book for forty years,

published journalistic columns on cookery which eventually
became popular cookbooks.

By 1880 more, and less expensive, cookbooks were
pouring into a literate and widespread American market.
The trend was toward cooking schools.   During the 1860s
Pierre Blott conducted his famous French School of cookery
in Boston and New York.   His lectures developed into a
1,000-recipe compilation, What to Eat, and How to Cook It
(1863).

The most famous of the cooking courses were taught
at the Boston Cookery School established by Mary Johnson
Lincoln.   Her text-book, Mrs. Lincoln's Boston Cook Book
(1884), sold well but was overshadowed by the Boston Cook-
ing-School Cook Book (1896) compiled by her successor, Fannie Merritt Farmer.   The recipes were not especially creative, but Fannie Farmer introduced the idea of standard and
precise measurements, thereby earning the gratitude of the
many novice cooks who have since made this cookbook a popular household item.   During the nineteenth century a large
immigrant population entered the U.S.   This gave a many-
sided character to American cookery and consequently made
it more difficult to define as American.   The owner of
the New York Cooking School, Mrs. Gesine Lemcke was
the best known author on German cookery.   The Philadelphia
Cookbook of Mrs. Rorer reflected the German cuisine of the
Pennsylvania area.   Lafcadio Hearn's classic La Cuisine
Creole, which appeared in 1895, gave another sort of insight
into regional American cookery.

Since 1895, cookbooks have been the most consistent
sellers in non-fiction in the U.S.   Although they encompass
one of the smallest categories of new books published annually,
they are among the most popular for the general public.   The

leading best seller among cookbooks, the Better Homes and
Gardens Cook Book, ranks second in the overall list of best
sellers during the past seventy years and first in the list of
best sellers available only in hardcover editions.   Encyclopedic texts such as Irma Rombauer's Joy of Cooking, the Settle-
ment Cookbook, the Betty Crocker Cookbook, the American
Woman's Cook Book, and the Gold Cook Book are a far cry
from the 47-page American Cookery by Amelia Simmons.
Since 1796 the American cookbook has evolved from a hodge-
podge pamphlet of recipes to a comprehensive, well organized, and carefully indexed work.

CONCLUSION

This concludes the preliminary discussion on the nature
and historical development of the literature of cookery and
gastronomy in the Western world. The reader is cautioned
to observe that this very brief survey of the culinary publications of Italy, France, Germany, England, Spain and the
United States is but a sketch based on secondary sources.
Any consideration of this topic should be supplemented and
expanded by a thorough study of original source material,
and by reference to historical and bibliographical commen-
taries, some of which are listed in the appendices. One
further caution:

> "Cookery is an art
> Still changing, and of momentary triumph.
> Know on thyself thy genius must depend.
> All books of cookery, all helps of art
> Are vain, if void of genius thou wouldst cook."
>
> --Julia Andrews,
> Breakfast, Dinner and Tea, 1859.

PART II

THE COLLECTIONS

INTRODUCTION

There are many cookbook collections held by universities, public libraries and private individuals within the United States. Lee Ash's Subject Collections (1974) lists 32 libraries under COOKERY, two libraries under GASTRONOMY, one under BEVERAGES, eight under WINE AND WINE MAKING, and 23 under FOOD. There are, without a doubt many others not listed or known.

This survey of culinary collections focuses on libraries selected: 1) in the hope that they might have historically important material; and 2) which could be visited within the three-month grant-leave of this project. Because of such limitations, it is not possible to claim either comprehensiveness or absolute accuracy. The inclusion of a collection in this study should not be interpreted to mean that it is "important" or that it is "historically oriented." Further, this study should not be interpreted to be either an historical treatise or abbreviated Vicaire with location symbols. Rather, it is an attempt:

1. to provide the potential researcher in the field of culinary arts with an indication of the range and variety of materials available in the United States;

2. to indicate the most probable location of materials which relate to his or her particular interest.

The following notes are, for the most part, the results of visits to selected libraries, personally viewing their

catalogs, shelf lists, or checklists, examining a few items
and discussing the collections with the curators and/or own-
ers. In some instances, a visit was not possible, but correspondence was received. Those libraries are identified
with the letters NV. There are almost no published mono-
graphs describing collections of culinaria. Usually materials
relating to cookery and gastronomy are described only briefly
via the library's catalog, if one exists. In the case of large
libraries, culinary material is most often scattered throughout total holdings and not isolated as a special collection.
The following, therefore, may serve only as a general guide
to the potential researcher. Information on specific items
must be obtained through direct correspondence with the
library or collector.

INDEX TO COLLECTIONS

The Collections 53

COLLECTIONS

Samford University Library
Birmingham, Alabama

Samford University Library has a collection of approximately 250 cookbooks in its Graduate Collection, mostly
English and American dating from the late 19th century to
the 1930s. There are no rare volumes. NV

University of California at Berkeley
The General Library
The Agriculture Library
The Bancroft Library
Berkeley, California

Culinary material at the University of California at
Berkeley is interfiled with books on other subjects in the
collections housed within the Main Campus Library, the Agriculture Library and the Bancroft Library (which holds early
northwestern United States material and Californiana). Of
particular historical interest are:

Bonnefons. Le Délices de la Campagne. 1617.
Scappi. Dell'Arte de Cucinare. 1643. Containing
Cervio's Il Trinciante and Pandini's Il Mastro di
Casa.
Apicius. De Re Coquinaria. 1542.
May, Robert. The Accomplisht Cook. 1660.
Der Verstandige Kock. 1668.
Le Manuel de la Friandise. 1797.
Works by: Beauvilliers, Carême, Soyer, Dubois,

> Menon, Moxon, Marin, Nott, Liger, Massialot,
> Warner, Bonnefons, Francatelli, Kitchner.
> Books on cookery published in California.

There are approximately 2,000 cookery books and
approximately 600 books on wine and wine making, including
several histories.   Of special note in the latter category are:
Alexander Henderson's History of Ancient and Modern Wines
(1824) and Edward Barry's Observations, Historical, Critical
and Medical on the Wines of the Ancients (1775).   There are
no special publications describing the culinary holdings of the
Berkeley Libraries; however, Liselotte Glozer's bibliography,
California in the Kitchen (1960), was compiled at the Bancroft Library.   This 43-page publication lists cookery books
published in California.   It is not complete; the Library of
Congress holds culinary materials published in California
which are not included in the Glozer bibliography.

City College of San Francisco
Alice Statler Library
San Francisco, California

The Alice Statler Library at the City College of San
Francisco opened in 1964.   It provides materials which sup-
port instruction in courses given in the Hotel and Restaurant
Department.   Over ninety per cent of the collection dates
from 1960.   There are no rare volumes, other than bound
magazines such as Hotel Monthly, 1897 through 1940; Western
Hotel Reporter 1906-, Volume 1 through Volume 82; Tavern
Talk 1910-, Volume 1 to date; Keeler's Pacific Hotel Review,
1919 through 1949.   Materials held are indicated via the
Alice Statler Library public catalog.

University of California at Davis
The University Library
Davis, California

The University of California at Davis has a large in-
structional program in wine technology. Emphasis is on
those works on viticulture and wines which will support current courses of instruction. There are reprints of classic
works on cookery and twentieth-century cookbooks within the
total collection. The Library holds approximately 50 cookbooks published before 1900, including: Novisimo Arte de
Cocina (Mexico, 1831): Francatelli's The Modern Cook (23rd
ed. , 1874); Carême's L'Art de la Cuisine Française au
Dix-neuvième Siècle, 1835; Raffald's The Experienced English
Housekeeper, 1786. Special collections include:

> Cebis Collection of 1,000 European wine labels, wine
> lists, menus, pamphlets and other related ephem-
> era.

> Wine Bottle Labels, collection of labels used between
> 1963 and 1968.

> Herrington Collection of menus.

Book holdings in the culinary arts are indicated through the
general public catalog.

The Private Collection of Mr. Paul Fritzche
San Rafael, California

A great many of the American regional and local cookbooks listed in Margaret Cook's America's Charitable Cooks
are to be found in this large private collection of over 10,000
volumes. In addition, there are many twentieth-century American publications in all areas of food preparation. Of special
note are several English cookery and household management

texts dating from the seventeenth and eighteenth centuries,
including:

> May's Accomplisht Cook. 1685.
> John Evelyn's Aceteria. 1679.
> The Queen's Closet Opened. 1678.
> The Lister Apicius of 1705.
> Lamb's Royal Cookery. 1710.
> La Chapell's Modern Cook. 1733.
> Briggs' The New Art of Cookery. 1744.
> Verral's Complete System of Cookery. 1759.
> Richardson's Science of Brewing. 1798.
> And the works of Glasse (several editions), Leslie,
>   Acton, Hale, Napier, Raffald, Eaton, Farley, Kid-
>   der.

The English authors are balanced by French writers
of the 1700s and 1800s including works by Viard, Beauvilliers,
Brisse, Menon, Massialot, Bernardi, Bonnefons, De la Reyniere, Ude, Dubuisson's L'Art du Distallateur (1779), Audi-
bert's L'Art Faire les Vin d'Imitation (1882) and the Traité
de Confiture (1689).

Also there are at least four rare Mexican cookbooks
of the 1800s, the Spanish Nuevo Art d'Cocino by Juan Altimaras (a 1767 edition), Darwin's Zoonomia (1796), the 1815
Poughkeepsie edition of American Cookery by Amelia Simmons, Mary Randolph's Virginia Housewife (1830), and more
than 20 manuscripts in Dutch, German and French, variously
dated in the mid-1700s.

The oldest items in the collection are:

> Athenae. Deiphnosophistaii. 1615. A quarto in
>   Greek and Latin text.
> Bruyerinis. De Re Cibaria. The 1600 Frankfort
>   edition.
> The 1590 Heidelberg edition of Ciaconnius' De Trin-
>   clino.
> A work by Marii Grapaldi Francisci dated 1533.
> Caelli Apetti. Mi Advlatricis. 1541.

There is no guide to the collection other than the

owner's author catalog.   Approximately 7,000 volumes will
be housed at Johnson and Wales College, Providence, Rhode
Island in the near future.

The Wine Museum of San Francisco
The Christian Brothers Collection
San Francisco, California

   The Wine Museum of San Francisco houses a collection
of about 1,000 volumes on wines and viticulture, including
works from 1550 to the present.   Included are:

   Penus, Ivris Civilis. Sive de Alimentis. 1550.
   Baccius, Andreae. De Naturali Vinorum. 1596.
   Traite sur la Nature ... de la Vigne. 1759.
   Chaptal. Traite Theoretique et ... Vigne. 1801.
   Dahlen, Heinrich Wilhelm. Die Wein Bereitung. 1878.
   Viala. Traité General de Viticulture; Ampelographie.
      1901-1910.
   Henderson. History of Ancient and Modern Wines.
      1824.
   Worlidge, J. Vinetum Britannicum or a Treatise of
      Cider. 1691.
   Ferrovillat, P. Les Celliers. 1896.
   De Guyenne, Colas. Le Manuel du Cultivateur ...
      d'Orleans. 1770.
   Barry, Edward. ... Wines of the Ancients. 1775.

The San Francisco Public Library   The Los Angeles Public
San Francisco, California   Library
                                    Los Angeles, California

   The collections of the San Francisco Public Library
and of the Los Angeles Public Library are up-to-date and intended for the use of the general public.   There are no rare
culinary works, but there are a few reprints of classic works
on cookery.   The public collections contain, for the most
part, popular, general and national cookbooks and books on
wines published since the 1940s.   The Los Angeles Public

Library has many modern Spanish language cookbooks, a copy
of Los Angeles Cookery (1881), and a copy of the 1732 Barcelona edition of Montiño's Arte de Concina.   The public
catalog serves as a guide to the material.

The San Diego Public Library
San Diego, California

        The San Diego Public Library houses a current ethnic
and general cookery collection.   There are a few 19th-cen-
tury titles of note, including: Catharine Beecher's American
Woman's Home, 1869; Mary Lincoln's Boston Cookbook,
1886; Marion Harland's (pseud. for Mary Terhune) Complete
Housewife's Guide, 1889. NV

Huntington Library
San Marino, California

        The Huntington Library is principally a conservatory
of works relating to British and American history and literature before 1900, as well as incunabula.   Culinary material
may be found within the scope of these holdings of five million manuscripts and over half a million books, by consulting
the public catalog. Of special note are: several editions of
Platina (1475, 1480, 1499, 1481, 1485, 1540, 1561); several
works of Claudius Galenus; the 1493 Basel edition of Magninus
Mediolanesis' Regimen Sanitatis; the Deipnosophistae of Athenaeus (1612) in Latin and Greek text; a 1500 edition of Apicius' De Re Coquinaria; the Sanitatis Salerniarum (1559) of
Arnaldus de Villa Nova, and the first edition of his De Vinus
(1478), the first printed book on wines.

The Hurty-Peck Library of Beverage Literature
The Collection of Mr. A. W. Noling
Irvine, California

The Hurty-Peck Library of Beverage Literature is a
collection of more than 6,000 items, principally written in
the English language. Included are materials principally relating to beverages: beer and brewing, cider and perry,
cocktails, cocoa and chocolate, flavorings, liquor, perfumery,
soft drinks, wine, etc. Included are a number of cookbooks
and books on food which "recommend themselves for their
close relation to beverage literature." Titles of note include:

> Acton, Eliza. Modern Cookery. 1860.
> Briggs, Richard. The New Art of Cookery. 1794.
> Gouffé, Jules. Book of Preserves. 1871.
> Kitchiner, William. Apicius Redivivus. 1817.
> Sanderson, J. M. Cook and Confectioner. 1849.
> Suzanne, Alfred. La Cuisine Anglaise. 1894.

Mr. Noling has published an 865-page bibliography,
Beverage Literature (Scarecrow Press, 1971), with location
symbols and an indication of the titles found in the Hurty-
Peck Library.

The Private Collection of Dr. Marcus Crahan
Los Angeles, California

This is an extensive and well-selected collection of
rare books on cookery, gastronomy, wines and related subjects. It is well indexed via a privately developed card catalog which indicates items not only by author, title and subject, but also by edition, date, type of illustrations, maps,
place of publication, provenance, etc. A bibliography is
presently in progress. Over 100 of the rarest items were
exhibited at the Bancroft Library in the Fall of 1975. The

catalog of this exhibit evidences the following titles of special
interest:

> Apicius. <u>Apicius Culinarius</u>. 1498. The first edition.
> Baccius, Andrea. <u>De Natvrali Vinorvm Historia</u>.
> (1596) The first issue.
> Beauvilliers, Antoine. <u>L'Art du Cuisinier</u>. 1814.
> The first edition, bound for the author.
> Corrado, Vincenzo. <u>Il Cuoco Galante</u>. 1773. The
> only recorded copy of the first edition.
> Crescenzi, Pietro de. <u>Ruralium Commodorum</u>. 1471.
> The first printed book on agriculture and economics.
> Escoffier, Auguste. <u>Le Guide Culinaire</u>. 1903. The
> only recorded copy of the first edition in French.
> Galenus, Claudius. <u>Galen's Calendar on Metus and
> Drynkys</u>. An illuminated manuscript on vellum,
> ca. 1420.
> Glasse, Hannah. <u>The Art of Cookery</u>. 1747.
> Katu, Ryuusui. <u>Um No Sachi</u>, 1762.
> La Varenne, Francois Pierre de. <u>Le Pastissier
> François</u>. 1655. The Elzevier edition.
> Messisbugo, Christoforo di. <u>Banchetti Compositioni</u>.
> 1549.
> Platina, Bartholomeo. <u>Platynae de Honesta Volvptate</u>.
> 1475.
> Scacchi, Franciscifabrianensis. <u>De Salvbri Potv Dis-
> sertatio</u>. 1622. The first edition of the earliest
> book on making sparkling wines.
> Schelhammer, Maria Sophia. <u>Die Wol Unterwiesene
> Kochinn</u> (1697) and <u>Der Wohl-unterwiesenen Kochinn
> Zufalliger Confecttisch</u>. (1699) An unrecorded first
> edition.
> Simmons, Amelia. <u>American Cookery</u>. The 1798
> Hartford edition.
> Villena, Don Henrique de Aragon, Marquis de. <u>Arte
> Cisoria</u>. 1766.

E. and J. Gallo Winery Library
Modesto, California

Most of the 6,000 works on or relating to wine at the
Gallo Winery Library are technically-oriented recent items
cataloged in a conventional manner. They are intended for
the use of company researchers and staff. There are no rare
items.

California State University, Fresno
Fresno, California

    The Viticulture and Oenology collection at California
State University, Fresno was assembled by a private collector
and became a part of the University's special collections in
1968. It contains 3,000 items, approximately half of which
are books. The collection includes 70 per cent of the U.S.
titles listed in L. H. Bailey's bibliography of wine and grape
books in his Evolution of Our Native Fruits (New York, 1898).
    Of special interest are:

    Estienne, Charles. Vineto. Venice. 1545.
    Redi, Francesco. Bacco in Toscana. Florence.
      1685.
    Charleton, Walter. Of the Mysterie of Vintners.
      England. 1669.

    The collection is uncataloged. There is no published
guide; however, a checklist of pre-1921 imprints and a descriptive bibliography of pre-1851 imprints are presently
being compiled. The collection was described in Wines and
Vines Magazine, October 1968, and in the November 1975
issue of the Journal of the International Wine and Food Society. NV

Yale University
Sterling Memorial Library
Beineke Rare Book and Manuscript Library
New Haven, Connecticut

    The Beineke Rare Book and Manuscript Library at
Yale University holds about 100 cookery texts among its
400,000 volumes. Titles of note include:

    Platina, Bartolomeo. De Honesta Voluptatae. Venice,
      1475.
    La Pratique de Faire Toutes Confitures. 1558.

Willich, Jodocus. Ars Magirica. 1563.
Messisbugo, Cristoforo. Libro Novo. 1556.
Woolley, Mrs. Hannah. The Gentlewoman's Companion.
   1673; The Accomplish'd Lady's Delight, 1677; The
   Queen-Like Closet, 1672.
Kent, Elizabeth (Talbot) Grey. A Choice Marval of
   Rare and Select Secrets, 1653.
Rundell. A New System of Domestic Cookery. 1817.

The catalog of the Sterling Library lists some 25 titles under
COOKERY--EARLY WORKS TO 1800. A few of these are
recent reprints; however, here one can also find the works
of Richard Briggs, Francis Collingwood, William Ellis,
Louise Friedel, Hannah Glasse, Edward Kidder, William
King, Vincent La Chapelle, Patrick Lamb, Samuel Pegge,
Menon, Audot, Nignon and Bartolomeo Stefani's L'Arte di
Ben Cucinare, 1671.

Emory University
Atlanta, Georgia

Emory University holds a miscellaneous collection of
cookery books numbering approximately 675 volumes. There
are no rare works. NV

Georgia College
Ira Dillard Russell Library
Milledgeville, Georgia

Georgia College holds a collection of approximately
300 cookbooks, mostly of recent publication. There are no
rare works. NV

The John Crerar Library
Chicago, Illinois

One of the great collections of rare and historically

important works on the culinary arts is housed in the John
Crerar Library.   The main collection includes many English,
French and German titles including those of Rabisha, Kent,
Kettibly, La Chapelle, Briand, Verral, Glasse, Briggs, Run-
dell, Farley, Farmer, Lemcke, Gouffé, Menon.   Especially
important titles include:

> Bruyerin-Champieri, Jean Baptiste.   De Re Cibaria
>   Libri XXII, 1560.
> Apicius.   De Re Culinaria.   Combined with Platina.
>   De Tuenda Valetudina, libri X.   1541.
> Scappi, Bartolomeo.   Opera.   Venice, 1596.
> Novismo Arte de Cocina.   Mexico, 1831.

And three unusual Japanese titles:

> Reigetsu-an, pseud.   Kasen Ryori, Tokyo, Izumoji,
>   1748.
> Tokusoshi, pseud.   Shinsen Kaiseki Skippoku Shukocha.
>   Tokyo, Suharays, 1771.
> Daigo, Sanjin, Ryor-Hayashinam Taizen, Tokyo, 1801.

The hidden wealth of this library, however, lies in
the vault which contains the Levis collection of approximately
500 works--each and every one a gem in culinary bibliography.
There are only a few scattered cards in the public catalog to
indicate some of the titles.   The books are cataloged but not
classified.   They are arranged by date of publication and the
corresponding shelf list, containing cataloger's descriptions,
is housed along with the collection itself.   Beginning with no
less than five editions of Platina, all issued prior to 1500
(both the Venice 1475 and the undated Rome edition), the
shelves hold sixteenth-century German, Italian, Latin and a
few French titles, including works of Apicius, Mediolano,
Cervvio, Colle, Elyot, Hubner, Romoli, Staindl, Rumpolt;
many health and medical treatises of the 1500s, including
quite a few works of Galen, several editions of Rosselli's
Epulario, Savonarola's Libretto ... Physico, 1515 and a rare

Paris 15-? edition of Taillevant (31 leaves).

The seventeenth century is also represented by many titles, including the Court and Kitchen of Elizabeth, Commonly called Joan Cromwell, L'Escole ..., Evelyn's Acetaria, Domingo Hernandez de Maceras' Libro del Arte de Cozina, 1607, several editions of the works of La Varenne, and writings by Gervase Markham, John Murrell, Massialot, John Shirley and Hannah Woolley.

The eighteenth century continues with the works of Altimaras, Susannah Carter, Lamb, Liger, Marin, Menon, Pegge, several editions of Hannah Glasse, including both the first and second editions of 1747. There are, additionally, several manuscripts including a 140-page ms: "De'pense de la bouche du roy Louis XIV. xx dern. annees. Paris, 17-?"

The nineteenth century includes Appert, Berchoux, Brillat-Savarin, Gouffé, Raffald, Rundell, a few books on the history of wines and viticulture and curiously, only one work of the great Carême.

The beginning of the twentieth century is represented by Pichon's work on Taillevent, Guegan's Apicius, the works of Vicaire, Boulestin, Eustis, Babinski.

This is truly a remarkable collection. Let us hope that the shelf list may someday be printed for researchers as a guide to its contents.

Newberry Library
Chicago, Illinois

The Newberry Library has approximately 100 titles relating to the culinary arts, mostly from the 1800s (Child, Furnivall, Gouffé, Napier, Hale, etc.). Within the catalog

are listed: a 1541 Apicius; a 1549 and a 1617 edition of
Messisbugo's Banchetti; a 1530 Paris edition of Platina; a
1556 Athenaeus in Latin; and a 1680 Athenaeus in French.

The Private Collection of Chef Louis Szathmary
Chicago, Illinois

The private collection of Chef Szathmary is an eclectic
mixture of over 5,000 exotic, ordinary and rare volumes on
cookery and gastronomy. It also includes more than 20,000
assorted pamphlets, menus, prints, etc. relating to the culinary arts. The collection ranges from a hand-illustrated
manuscript of a book on carving by Pierre Petit, L'Art de
Trancher la Viande, 1646, to Nantuckett Receipts of 1874, to
recent books on African cookery, to a 1791 Spanish work
listed as Arte de Treposteria by Juan de la Mata, to Carving and Serving by Mrs. D. A. Lincoln, 1886, to several
rare printed Hungarian receipt books, to ten or more German
manuscripts of the 16th-17th centuries, to American charitable groups cookbooks, to the 19th century works of Carême,
Dubois, Gouffé, Viard, and Grimod de la Reyniere. Of special note are:

> Ciacconius. De Trinclino. 1588.
> Cervio's Il Trinciante. 1593 and 1581.
> Von Rumpolt's Ein New Kockbuch. 1587.
> Massonio, Salvatore. Archidipno Overo dell'in
>   Salata. 1627.
> Libri de re Rustica. 1533.
> Lister's 1709 Apicius.
> A 1556 edition of the Dipnosophistarum.
> A ms. cookbook written in Latin, German and Hun-
>   garian, ca. 1490-1530.
> Ciccarelli, Alphonso. Opuscuium de Tuberibus. 1564.
> Staindl von Dillingen, Balthassar. Ein Kunstliches ...
>   Kochbuch. 1545.
> Villena. Arte Cisoria. 1766.

Ryff, Gaultherus.   Confect-buch.   1563.
Gilliers.   Le Cannaméllist Français.   1751.

A brief article on this collection appeared in the April
1974 issue of American Libraries and another in the New York
Times, July 10, 1972.   There is no guide to the collection
other than an author catalog developed by the owner.

Indianapolis-Marion County Public Library
Indianapolis, Indiana

The Indianapolis Public Library holds a large circulating
cookbook collection and a special collection originally consisting
of about 75 volumes gathered by Mr. Wright Marble.   The collection contains a number of 17th- and 18th-century English
and Italian works, along with German, French, English titles
published in the 19th century.   The library also houses the
Arthur Stumpf collection of about 100 menus.   NV

Kansas State University
Farrell Library, Manhattan, Kansas

The Farrell Library of Kansas State University has approximately 3,000 cookery books, 800 of which are shelved in
Special Collections.   American, English and German household
manuals dominate.   A 230-page bibliographic catalog of this
collection was published as Kansas State University Receipt
Book and Household Manual, compiled by G. A. Rudolph, 1968.
Of special note are: Scappi's Opera, 1570; and some 40 English
works published in the 1600s, including:

1649.   Regimen Sanitatis Salerni, or the School of
           Salernes Regiment of Health.
1654.   A Choice Manual ... Rare and Select Secrets
           ... Countess of Kent.

1654.   A Closet for Ladies.
1655.   The Queen's Closet Opened.
1656.   The English Housewife.
1664.   The Court and Kitchen of Elizabeth.
1665.   The Accomplisht Cook.
1669.   The Closet of ... Sir Kenelme Digbie.
1670.   The Queen-Life Closet.
1682.   The Whole Body of Cookery Dissected.
1690.   The Young Cooks Monitor.

United States Department of Agriculture
National Agricultural Library, Beltsville, Maryland

The National Agricultural Library has uncounted numbers of items on cookery and gastronomy among its 1,500,000
volumes which pertain to agriculture and its related fields.
There is no separate listing, but items may be found through the
National Agriculture Library catalog published in 1973.   There
is also a mimeographed "Selected List of Historic Books on
Cookery in the National Agricultural Library."   Titles of note
include:

Accum.   Culinary Chemistry.   1821.
Apicius ... De Re Culinaria ... Platinae ... Pavli
      Eginetae De Facultatibus, 1541.
Carter.   The Compleat City and Country Cook.   1736.
The Family Magazine.   1741.
Jarrin.   The Italian Confectioner.   1823.
Kettilby.   A Collection of Above Three Hundred Receipts.
      1719.
Latini.   Lo Scalo.   1692.
Moxon.   English Housewifry.   1749.
Nonnius.   Diaeteticon Sive de Re Cibaria.   1646.
Randolph.   The Virginia Housewife.   1830.
Smith.   Court Cookery.   1725.
NV

United States Department of Health, Education and Welfare
Public Health Service, National Institute of Health
National Library of Medicine, Bethesda, Maryland

The National Library of Medicine houses an extensive
collection of materials on gastronomy and allied subjects.   In
Cleveland, Ohio in 1948, an exhibit was held of early books on
food and drink from the Army Medical Library.   After World
War II, the books were returned to the National Library of Medicine.   The check list for this exhibit mentions:

Platina.   De Honesta Voluptate.   Venice, 1475.
Platina.   Von Allen Speisen und Gerichten.   Strass-
    burg, 1530.
Ryff.   New Kochbuck für die Kranken.   Frankfurt am
    Main, 1555.
Bruyerin.   De Re Cibaria Libri XXII.   Lyon, 1560.
Pisanelli.   Trattato Della Natura de Cibi et del Bere.
    Venice, 1584.
Massonio.   Archidipno ... Insalata.   Venice, 1627.
Wecker.   New Köstlich und Nützliches Kochbuch.
    Basel, 1652.
La Chapell.   The Modern Cook.   1744.
Leméry.   A Treatise ... 1745.
Parmentier.   Recherches sur les Végétaux.   1781.
Dufour.   Traitez ... du Café.   Lyon, 1685.
Accum.   A Treatise ... Wine.   1820.

A search of the Index-Catalogue of the Library Surgeon General's Office under appropriate subject headings indicates
that there are other important culinary titles, including 17th-
and 18th-century English household texts.   Also, culinary
titles are listed in:

A Catalog of Sixteenth Century Printed Books in the
    National Library of Medicine, 1967.

Schullian-Sommer.   A Catalog of Incunabula and Manu-
    scripts in the Army Medical Library, 1950.
NV

University of Massachusetts Library
Amherst, Massachusetts

The Carolyn Maddox Beard collection of approximately

100 titles received in the early 1960s was integrated into the
general circulating collection. Items are predominantly American works published in the late 19th and early 20th centuries.
NV

American Antiquarian Society
Worcester, Massachusetts

The collection of the American Antiquarian Society
focuses on materials printed in new world English colonies
and the United States through the year 1876. The first American cookbook, American Cookery by Amelia Simmons, and a
few wine books are here, along with most other cookery
books published in the United States before 1821. There are
also a few post-1821 imprints. Holdings of over 650 cookery
items are listed in the bibliography American Cookery Books,
1742-1860, issued by the Society.

Harvard University Libraries
Cambridge, Massachusetts

Since the majority of Harvard's 1,500 books on household management were transferred to Radcliffe College in
1961, only a very few English items of the 17th and 18th
centuries remain listed in the Widener Library catalog. The
Houghton Rare Books Library lists a few under cookery, including:

> Beeton, Isabella. Beeton's Book of Household Manage-
>   ment. 1859-61.
> Brillat-Savarin, Anthelme. Physiologie du Goût. 1826.
> Carter, Susannah. The Frugal Housewife. 1796.
> L'Escole Parfaite des Officiers de Bouche. 1662.
> Plat, Sir Hugh. Diuers Chemicall Conclusions. 1694.
> Platina, Bartolomeus. Platina de Honesta Voluptatae.
>   1508.

Pullan, Matilda. The Modern Housewife's Receipt
    Book. 1854.
Rosselli, Giovanni. Opera Noua Chiamata Epulario.
    1516.
Brooks, Catherine. The Complete English Cook.
    1767.
The Compleat Cook. 1658.
Grant, Elizabeth Rapier. The Receipt Book of. 1924.
Murrel, John. A Daily Exercise for Ladies. 1617.
The Queen's Closet Opened. 1658.
Woolley, Hannah. The Gentlewoman's Companion.
    1673.
King, William. The Art of Cookery. 1708.
La Gastronome Francais. 1828.
LaRoche, Henry Jean. Cuisine. 1935.
Messisbughi, Christoforo di. Banchetti Compositioni
    di Vivande. 1549.
Scappi, Bartolomeo. Opera. 1596.

Radcliffe College
Schlesinger Library
Cambridge, Massachusetts

Within the Schlesinger Library, dedicated to the History of Women in America, there is a special collection of
over 3,000 titles on household management, cookery and
gastronomy. The emphasis is on works published by American women and modern well-known food writers, male and
female. Additionally, there are many English and French
texts, primarily from the 18th and 19th centuries. This collection was obtained, for the most part, from the transfer of
the home economics section of Harvard University in 1961,
and from the private library of Samuel and Narcissa Chamber-
lain. The papers of Julia Child and M. F. K. Fisher are
soon to be a part of the collection. Items of special interest
include:

1795. Susannah Carter's The Frugal Housewife.
1754. The Family Magazine.

1862. Francatelli, Charles. A Plain Cookery Book.
1774. Glasse, Hannah. Art of Cookery.
1887. Lincoln, Mary. Boston School Kitchen Text
        Book.
1774. Adam's Luxury and Eve's Cookery.

There is no guide to the collection other than entries
in the public catalog.

Detroit Public Library
Detroit, Michigan

The Gifts and Rare Books Division of the Detroit Public Library holds a largely uncataloged collection of over
1,500 cookery books presented to the Library, for the most
part, by Doris Patten and Fred Sanders. Most titles are
18th- and 19th-century British and American imprints and a
few French. Emphasis is on American items since 1850.
Included are several interesting regional items:

    Dieters, Rean. Hollandsche Kookerij. Holland, Mich-
      igan, 1936.
    Harvest Festival Cook Book. Fall River, Massachu-
      setts, 7th ed. , 1896.
    Mohawk Valley Cookbook. Canajoharie, New York,
      1906.
    Squire, Emily. A Collection of Choice Recipes.
      Westfield, Mass. 1884.
    Mumford. Genessee Valley Cookbook. Boston, 1905.
    Carolina Housewife. 1847.
    Harland, Ester. The New England Economical House-
      keeper. 1847.

Included are works by Accum, Acton, Lister, Audot,
Beauvilliers, Beecher, Beeton, Briggs, Brillat-Savarin,
Dumas, Farley, Berchoux, Glasse, Kettilby, La Chapelle,
Lamb, Leslie, King, Lee, Lincoln, Nutt, Peggee, Raffald,
Rabisha, Rundell. There is also a 1498 Venice edition of
Platynae De Honesta Voluptate.

The main Library has a modest circulating collection
of popular, modern cookbooks.

Michigan State University Library
East Lansing, Michigan

Michigan State University Library, Special Collections
Division houses approximately 400 cookery titles published
prior to 1900, mostly 19th-century English language items.
A mimeographed listing of holdings mentions, among others:

> Beauvilliers. The Art of French Cookery. London,
>   1824.
> Briggs, Richard. The New Art of Cookery. Phila-
>   delphia, 1792.
> Burr, Hattie. The Woman Suffrage Cook Book. 1886.
> Carter, Susannah. The Frugal Housewife, 1792.
> The Cook Not Mad. 1831.
> The Cook's Own Book. 1832.
> Evelyn, John. Acetaria. 1699.
> Gelleroy, William. London Cook. 1762.
> Lamb, Patrick. Royal Cookery. 1716.
> Randolph, Mary. The Virginia Housewife. 1838.
> Simmons, Amelia. American Cookery. Poughkeepsie,
>   1815.
> True Gentlewoman's Delight. 1659.
> Worlidge, J. Vinetum Britannicum or a Treatise of
>   Cider. 1691.

The oldest title is a copy of the 1541 Basle edition of
Apicius' De Re Culinaria. A collection of over 800 current
cookery titles used in connection with curricular studies in
the School of Hotel, Restaurant and Institutional Management
is also housed in the Special Collections Division.

The Private Collection of Mrs. Howard H. Peckham
Ann Arbor, Michigan

This private collection includes approximately 200

American imprints, most from the 19th century. About 30
items are charitable cookbooks and 45 trade or advertising
cookbooks.   There are also several manuscript cookbooks,
one of which dates before 1800. <u>NV</u>

Saint John's University
Hill Monastic Manuscript Library
Collegeville, Minnesota

   This library is included in this survey because of
what it promises to offer. Established in 1964, its dual
function is to preserve on microfilm handwritten manuscripts
dating before 1600 which are still extant in European monas-
teries and allied libraries and to make these resources available to interested users in the United States.   To date, over
32,000 codices and 100,000 papyri held in 75 Austrian libraries have been filmed.   Also filmed to date are more than
6,000 codices from libraries in Spain; nearly 3,000 volumes
of manuscript material from Malta; and, over 6,000 codices
from Ethiopia.   The <u>American Journal of Enology and Viti-
culture</u>, Vol. 25, No. 1, 1974 published a preliminary listing of manuscript materials on the subject of wine and wine
making which were filmed.   There are also a few culinary
texts presently on film, including

> Göttweig. <u>Kuchenmaistery</u>. 1525.
> Saltzburg <u>MS.</u> On fols. 255-318 is a <u>Kochbuch</u>, part
> of a larger work by Johannes Jacobi titled <u>Liber
> qui Dicitur Secretarium.</u>
> Sankt Florian MS XI.   <u>Liber Coquinarius.</u>
> Innsbruch. MS. <u>Kuchenmeistery.</u>

<u>NV</u>

The Minneapolis Public Library
Minneapolis, Minnesota

The Minneapolis Public Library has a popular circulating cookbook collection and cook books of local or regional interest (church groups, societies, organizations, etc.). The Minnesota section of Margaret Cook's America's Charitable Cooks indicates the type of material held. NV

The Private Collection of Mrs. Ester B. Aresty
Princeton, New Jersey

This private collection of over 500 volumes on the culinary arts contains classics carefully selected for their importance and their mint condition. There is an English-language emphasis, although a few French and a scattering of Italian, American, German and Spanish works are also included. There are also several English-language manuscripts, principally Elizabethan. Many of the items held are described in The Delectable Past (1964), written by Mrs. Aresty. Of special interest are:

Athenaeus. The Deipnosophists. Aldine Press, 1514.
Weckerin, Anna. Kochbuch.
Brillat-Savarin. Physiologie du Goût. The illustrated
    Bertall edition of 1868 and the first edition, 1826.
The Elsevier edition of Le Pastissier François.
Il Cuoco Piemontese. 1767.
A 1789 Russian cookbook.
La Mata. Arte de Reposteria. 1747.
Platina. De Honesta Voluptatae. A 1475 Latin edition
    and a 1501 Italian edition.
Kidder, E. D. Receipts of Pastry and Cookery. Un-
    dated. This copy has a printed title page and the
    rest is handwritten; similar to a copy held by the
    John Crerar Library.
American Cookery by Amelia Simmons, the Walpole,
    N. H. edition of 1812; a copy which belonged to
    D. A. Lincoln.
N. H. Bailey's Household Dictionary; Dictionarium
    Domesticum. 1736.

The New York Academy of Medicine
New York, New York

The New York Academy of Medicine holds one of the
rarest culinary items in the world, a 9th-century manuscript
on vellum (58 leaves) of De Re Culinaria Libri I-IX by Apicius. (There is only one other surviving manuscript, held
by the Vatican Library.) There are also a 1503, a 1541,
and other editions of Apicius. Other rare items include:

> Stefani, B. L'Arte di Ben Cucinare, 1635.
> Der Frantzösische Becker und der Frantzösische Kock.
>   1677.
> Bruyerin. De Re Cibaria. 1560 and 1600.
> Platina. 1498 and 1541.
> Frugoli. Practica e Scalcaria. 1631.
> Von Rumpolt. 1581.
> Scappi. 1596.
> Di Messisbugo. 1549 and 1610.
> Egerin, Susanna. Leipziger Kockbuch. 1732.
> Rosselli. Epulario. 1674, 1682, 1750.
> Yüan, Mei. Süi-yüan shih tan, 1792. A work by the
>   Brillat-Savarin of China.
> Rodrigues, Domingos. Arte de Cozinha, 1693. Writ-
>   ten by the Chef to the King of Portugal.
> Works by Carême, Menon, Massialot, Beauvilliers,
>   Viard, Francatelli, Soyer, Brisse, Audot, Corrado.

There are also modern books on various kinds of diets.
An informally arranged "cards and slips listing books, pamphlets, etc. on cookery, food, etc. given to the New York
Academy of Medicine by Dr. Margaret Barclay Wilson. 2
catalog drawers in S. closet" exists and, in addition to the
public catalog, serves as a guide to culinary material. The
researcher may also consult The New York Academy of Medicine. Subject Catalog of the Library published by G. K.
Hall, Boston, 1969.

Cornell University
School of Hotel Administration
Howard B. Meek Library
Ithaca, New York

The Howard B. Meek Library contains over 18,000
volumes intended for the use of students, faculty and alumni
of the Cornell School of Hotel and Business Administration.
There are two special collections relating to the culinary
arts: The J. B. Herndon collection of 1,500 volumes, mostly
late 19th- and early 20th-century materials with a few manuscripts and other rare items; and the Joseph D. Vehling collection of approximately 500 titles from the 15th through the
early 20th century.   There are several rare books on carving by Petit, Procacchi, Giegher, Sweerts and Kletten.   More
than one-third of the older German language titles included
in this collection are quite rare and not traceable in the
usual culinary bibliographies:

Ramingen. <u>Von den Aromaten</u>. 1580. A treatise on
    spices.
Corvinus. <u>Frauenzimmer Lexicon</u>, 1715, and Reichen-
    bach, 1793; cookery dictionaries.
<u>Nürnbergisches Kochbuch</u>, 1734.
Cesare Evitascandalo's four volumes on the manage-
    ment of a noble Renaissance household.
Ottaviano Rabasco. <u>Il Convito</u>. A handbook on ban-
    quets, their history, organization, etc.
<u>Ordonnance Surles Faicts du Meistier de Cuisinier
    ... Bayeaux</u>. A ms. begun in 1472 and discon-
    tinued in 1711.
<u>Etat et Menus de la Maison du Roi</u>, 1748. A manu-
    script account book from the household of Louis XV.
<u>Kochbuch von Balthasar Staindl von Dillingen</u>.
<u>Oberrheinische Kochbuch</u>. 3rd. ed. The oldest gas-
    tronomic work from the province of Alsace.
<u>Livlandisches Kochbuch</u>. From the Baltic Sea coun-
    tries.
<u>Hollandasche Keuken Meid</u>. Dutch dishes of the 18th
    century.
<u>Swedisches Kockbuch</u>. A German edition of 1789.

Two 16th-century German manuscripts of considerable
   size (316 and 500 pages respectively).
Aegidius Albertinus. Zwey Schöne Träctatl, Munich,
   1598. Containing Antonio de Guevara's critique of
   Spanish life.
Apicius, Basel edition of 1541 and a Lyon edition of
   the same year.
LaVarenne. Le Cuisinier Francois. 1654.

These two special collections are cataloged and shelved
in a special room. The shelf list is included in the general
shelf list of the library. J. D. Vehling's checklist of his
collection is interfiled as a typewritten manuscript within
that collection. There is an excellent mimeographed evaluation of the collection written by S. Vinceus and a list of selected materials from the Vehling collection. An exhibit of
a few of the rarer items was held at the National Food,
Cookery and Allied Trades Exposition in 1931; the catalog
for the exhibit was published in Hotel Bulletin and The Na-
tions Chefs magazine of the time.

The New York Historical Society Library
New York, New York

The New York Historical Society Library holds a few
cookery manuscripts and texts within its collections on American history. The first edition of American Cookery and the
1798 edition are included. The Arnold Shircliffe menu collection is housed here as well as a collection of historical
materials on hotels, taverns, restaurants and theatres in
New York prior to 1942, gathered by W. Johnson Quinn.

The New York State Historical Association
Copperstown, New York

The Beaumont Newhall Cookbook Collection of 226 vol-

umes is the core of the cookery collection, which totals approximately 300 volumes relating to the late 18th and the
19th centuries.   There are English, French, German and
Italian works.   Additionally there is a small manuscript collection of original receipt books.   NV

Fred C. Taylor Memorial Library
Hammondsport, New York

        This is a private library of 1500 volumes relating to
wine and wine making.   It is uncataloged.   NV

The New York State Library
State Education Department
Albany, New York

        The New York State Library holds a collection of
books relating to American cookery, mostly published in the
late 19th and 20th centuries.   All cookbooks printed before
1860 are listed in the American Cookery Books bibliography
of the American Antiquarian Society.   NV

The Pierpont Morgan Library
New York, New York

        The Pierpont Morgan Library holds several titles re-
lating to the culinary arts within its 70,000 volume collection
on early printed works, including:

> Hispalensis, Isidorus. Etymologiae, 1472.   An ency-
>   clopedia originally written by the Bishop of Seville
>   (c. 560-636).   It includes information on food,
>   drinks and cooking utensils.
> Apicius. De Re Coquinaria.   Medolani, 1498.   First
>   edition.
> Cato, Marcus Porcius, Censorius ... De Re Rustica.

Venice, 1472.   First edition of life on a Roman
estate in 2nd century; some cooking recipes.

Curtius, Matthaeus.   De Prandii ac Cenae Modo Libel-
lus, 1566.

Evelyn, John.   Acetaria.   1699.   1st edition.

Glasse, Hannah.   The Art of Cookery 1749--an uncut
1st edition.

Greenhough, Thomas.   Cookery Medicinal Recipes.
Ms. 1699.

Liger, Louis.   La Nouvelle Maison Rustique, 1721.

Le Pastissier François.   Amsterdam, 1655.

Platina, Bartolomeus.   De Honesta Voluptate.   Editions: 1475 Venice, [1474?] Rome, 1480, 1487,
1499.

Nyland, Peter.   Den Ervaren Huys-houder.   Amsterdam, 1670.   Bound with Jan van der Groen's Den
Nederlandtscher Hovenier, 1670 (on pp. 57-88 of
which is De Verstandige Kock).

Roberts, I.   The Young Cook's Guide.   London, 1836.

Plat, Sir Hugh.   Delights for Ladies.   1632.

Markham, Gervase.   The English House-wife.   1637.

Beeton, Isabella.   The Book of Household Management.
1861.

Soyer, Alexis.   The Gastronomic Regenerator.   1846.

Giegher, Mattia.   Li Tre Trattati ... Padova.   1639.

Athenaeus.   Deipnosophists.   1514.   A Greek text.

The Culinary Institute of America
The Katharine Angell Library
Hyde Park, New York

The Katharine Angell Library houses approximately
15,000 volumes intended to support a two-year concentrated
program in cookery and food services.   Most titles are 20th-
century texts on foods, beverages and restaurant management.
There is a separate collection of approximately 1,000 rare
works dating from the 16th through the 19th centuries.   The
bulk of these are French classics, originally collected by
Chef Camille Jaget.   Included are the works of La Varenne,
Carême, Escoffier, Gouffé, Beauvilliers, Audot, Bonnefons,
Brillat-Savarin, Dubois, Dumas, Grimod de la Reyniere,

Liger, Marin, Menon, Massialot, Viard. Of special note
are:

> Athenaeus. Dipnosophistarum. 1556.
> Athenaeus. Le Quinze Livres. 1680.
> Bruyerinus. De Re Cibaria. 1560.
> Ciacconius. De Triclinio. 1644.
> Platina. Les Dix Livres. 1560.
> Mediolanesis. Regimen Sanitatis. 1503.
> Carême, Antonin. L'Art de la Cuisine Francaise.
>> 1843.
>> Le Cuisinier Parisien. 1842.
>> Le Maître D'Hôtel. 1842.
>> Le Pâtissier Pittoresque. 1828.
>> Le Pâtissier Royal Parisien. 1841.
>> Le Principal de la Cuisine De Paris. 1844.
> Escoffier, Auguste. Les Fleurs en Cire. 1910.
>> Le Guide Culinaire. 1911.
>> Le Livre des Menus. 1912.
>> Ma Cuisine. 1934.
> Krafft, Michael. The American Distiller. 1804.
> Lemery. A Treatise of All Sorts of Foods. 1745.
> Viala. Ampelographie. 1910.

There is a mimeographed author listing of rare items.
Reprints, historical texts, etc. are detailed in the public
catalog.

The Private Collection of Eleanor Lowenstein
New York, New York

Most of the cookery titles mentioned in André Simon's
Bibliotheca Gastronomica are in this private collection of
nearly a thousand items, most of which were obtained from
André Simon. Titles originally contained in Simon's collection have been supplemented with first editions or more valu-
able editions, plus culinary titles not originally owned by
Simon. The writings of La Varenne are here in several edi-
tions--a Lyon edition of 1680, 1660, 1659, 1699 Brussels,
1654 English translation, 1690 in Italian, and others. There

are at least nine different editions of Hannah Glasse including
a 1747 edition with a portrait of the author.   Amelia Sim-
mon's American Cookery is here in the 1814 Vermont edition
and the 1808 edition.   Most of the French and English culinary classics (Carême, Lamb, Verral, Briggs, Rundell) are
here including much from the 17th century:

1628.	Venner. Via Recta ad Vitam Longam.
1623.	Markham. Country Contentments or the English Housewife.
1609.	De la Casa. Le Galatée.
1650.	Murrel's Two Bookes of Cookerie and Carving.
1670.	Hannah Woolley. Queen-like Closet.
1634.	Lvcerna de Corteggiani.
1684.	Bonnefons. Les Delices de la Campagne.
1682.	Susannah Carter. A True Gentlewoman's Delight.
1651.	John French. The Art of Distillation.
1653.	Hugh Plat. The Jewel House of Art and Nature.
1682,	Rabisha. The Whole Body of Cookery Dissected.
1669.	Digby. The Closet of Sir Kenelm Digby.
1662.	Francisco Martinez Montiño. Arte de Cocina.
1682.	Muret. Traite des Festins.

Older and rarer works include:

Athenaeus.   A 1535 Greek edition.
Platina.   A 1499 Bologna and a 1475 Venice edition.
Scappi.   Opera.   Venice, 1510.
Apicius.   Coquinaria.   A 1500 Venice edition.

A tiny gem is a manuscript with crude colored draw-
ings, Trenchir Buechlers, from the collection of Fred W.
Scheibe.

There is no guide or index to the collection other than
the Simon bibliography.

The New York Public Library
New York, New York

The New York Public Library holds a wide assortment

of culinary material both recent and rare, from modern popular cookbooks to a scattering of the classics in culinary
fields.   There is one separate collection: The culinary collection of Helen Hayes Whitney, containing over 200 printed
cookery books, largely English, ranging from the 15th to the
20th centuries.   The majority of other materials are from
the 17th and 18th centuries.   The gem of the collection is a
15th-century manuscript compilation of recipes similar to
those found in the Forme of Cury and other manuscripts
edited by Samuel Pegge in 1780.   A published guide, The
Whitney Cookery Collection, is available from the New York
Public Library.

      Additionally, a check of the library catalogs indicates
that the Rare Books Division holds, among other titles:

A 1655 Elzevier edition of Le Pastissier François.
La Varenne.   Le Cuisinier, 1654, and French, Italian
      and English editions of this work published in the
      17th century.
Apicius.   1542 and 1541.
Granado, Maldona de Diego.   Libro del Arte de Co-
      zina, 1609.
Evitascandalo.   Libro dello scalo, 1609, 1627.
Massonio, Salvatore.   Archidipno, 1627.
Messisbugo.   Banchetti, 1557.
Scappi.   Opera, 1610.
Pisanelli.   Trattato Della Natura de Cibi, 1585 and
      1619.
Bruyerin.   De Re Cibaria, 1560.
A German edition of Platina, 1531.
Foster, John.   England's Happiness Increased, 1664.
Briggs.   New Art of Cookery, 1792.
Carter.   Frugal Housewife, 1796.
Beeton.   Book of Household Management, 1861.
Dawson, Thomas.   The Good Housewives Jewel, 1587.
Kent.   A Choice Manual, 1653.
Salmon, The Family Dictionary, 1696.
Emerson.   New England Cookery, 1808.
Randolph.   Virginia Housewife, 1824.
Eustis.   Cooking in Old Creole Days, 1904.

A Dictionary Catalog of the Rare Book Division of the

New York Public Library, published by G. K. Hall, may
also serve as a guide to culinary material.

Teachers College
The Russell Library
Columbia University
New York, New York

    The Russell Library houses over 1,000 cookery titles,
mostly English and American (plus a few French and German)
works from the 19th and very early 20th centuries.   Many
of the publications of the women who conducted cooking schools
and schools of domestic science are represented.   Additionally, there are rare and classic works:

> A Closet for Ladies and Gentlewomen.   1656.
> Le Pastissier François.   1655.
> Queen's Delight.   1679.
> Dictionnaire Portratif.   1772.
> Rosselli.   Opera ... Epulario.   1517.
> Salmon.   Family Dictionary.   1696.
> Scappi.   Opera.   1622.
> Schelhammer.   Der Wohl-unterwiesenen Kochin.   1699.
> Tillinghast.   Rare and Excellent Receipts.   1690.
> The Young Cooks Monitor.   1690.

> And the writings of Menon, Moxon, Nott, Raffald,
>> Massialot, Hall, La Chapell, Farley, Lamb, Woolley,
>> Dubois and others.

Cookery books are indicated in The Dictionary Catalog
of Teachers College Library, Columbia University, published
by G. K. Hall (1970).   Although no survey has been made of
the works mentioned, it would appear that many of the titles
should be listed in the American Cookery Books bibliography
of the American Antiquarian Society.

The University of North Carolina
Greensboro, North Carolina

The Special Collections Department of the University
of North Carolina holds approximately 140 volumes relating
to gastronomy and cookery, ranging in date from 1654 to
1952. There are two 17th-century imprints and several 18th-
century imprints. The main emphasis is the 19th century.
There is also an uncataloged collection of North Carolina
cookbooks. NV

The Cleveland Public Library
Cleveland, Ohio

The 8,000-volume cookbook collection of the Cleveland
Public Library is made up of 20th-century works, largely
dealing with ethnic or popular American cookery. A survey
of the public catalog indicates that there are no rare items
other than the Family Dictionary of William Salmon, 1705.

Case Western Reserve University Libraries
Cleveland, Ohio

The Special Collections Division of the University
Libraries holds approximately 300 volumes on wine and wine
making, most of which date from the early 20th century.
There are no rare items of culinary interest. NV

Ohio State University Libraries
Columbus, Ohio

The Home Economics Library collection is composed
of approximately 11,000 volumes intended to support the
Home Economics curriculum. Most of the material is cur-

rent. A dictionary catalog of holdings including culinary
materials will be published in the near future. NV

The Private Collection of Mrs. Thomas M. Scruggs
Held by Mrs. Margaret Cook
Kent, Ohio

More than half of the titles before 1831 listed in
American Cookery Books were in this collection which totaled
almost 3,000 volumes. Holdings included primarily English
and American works dating from the 17th, 18th and early
19th centuries as well as a few French titles and works in
other languages. There were also many American regional
cookbooks, primarily from western states. Of special note
was the Maurice Joyant La Cuisine de Monsieur Momo (1930),
with the original plates by Toulouse-Lautrec; Hannah Glasse,
The Art of Cookery (1747), and the first edition of Amelia
Simmons, American Cookery (1796).

A typewritten author list served as a guide to the
collection. There were also several subject lists, developed
by the owner. The collection was dispersed at auction in
September 1977.

The Private Collection of Mrs. Joseph Carson
Philadelphia, Pennsylvania

This is a private collection of books and manuscripts
relating to gastronomy and cookery. Items are early American imprints, principal emphasis being given to those published in or near Philadelphia. Interesting titles include:

Richard Briggs' New Art of Cookery, Philadelphia,
    1792.
Universal Receipt Book, Philadelphia, 1818.

Thomas Walker's The Art of Dining, Philadelphia, 1837.

Oeconomy oder Haushaltungskunst, Philadelphia, 1809.

Johann Kraus' Oeconomisches Haus- und Kunst Buch, Allentown, 1819.

Lucy Emerson's New-England Cookery, Montpelier, 1808.

Robert Roberts' The House Servant's Directory, Boston, 1827.

The Cook Not Mad, Watertown, New York, 1831.

Mary Coate's Book of Cookery, Philadelphia, 1740, MS.

Rebecca Dawson's Cookery Book, Philadelphia, c. 1790, MS.

There are also letters, handbills, menus, prints, etc. NV

Pennsylvania State University
The Fred Lewis Pattee Library
University Park, Pennsylvania

This collection of approximately 1,000 cookery titles, originally a part of the College of Home Economics, has been assimilated into the main library collection. Most are current references, with a few titles from the late 1800s. A bibliography compiled by Cordelia W. Swinton is available. NV

The Private Collection of Mary Tolford Wilson
Norwich, Vermont

This is a modest collection of almost 400 volumes. All are American imprints, with 1798 being the earliest. Included are works compiled by local charitable groups. NV

Colonial Williamsburg Foundation
Research Library
Williamsburg, Virginia

The Research Library of Colonial Williamsburg has a
small collection of 18th-century cookbooks, most of which
are known to have been in Virginia during that century. There
are also a few modern works dealing with early cookery and
reprints of scarce items. Items of note include:

    La Cuisinière Bourgeoise. 1769.
    Smith. The Complete Housewife. 1742.
    Harrison. The Housekeeper's Pocket Book. 1755.
    Randolph. Virginia Housewife. 1855 and 1824.
    Le Confiturier Royal. 1776.
    The Experienced Butcher. 1816.
    Farley. London Art of Cookery. 1804.
    Tyree. Housekeeping in Old Virginia. 1878.
    Glasse. Art of Cookery. 1760.
    Johnson. The Enterprising Housekeeper. 1898.
    Moxon. English Housewifery. 1789.
    Raffald. The Experienced English Housekeeper. 1755.
    Parmentier. Le Parfait Boulanger. 1778.
    Nutt. The Complete Confectioner. 1790.
    King. The Art of Cookery. 1708.

The Private Collection of Mr. and Mrs. Walter Husted
Alexandria, Virginia

This private collection of over 7,000 cookbooks contains 20 manuscripts, English and American, ranging from
1695 through the early 20th century; 287 early printed volumes,
English and American, from the 18th and 19th centuries, including Glasse, Simmons, Smith, Randolph; 1,389 regional
American cookbooks or charity cook books, dating from the
mid-19th century; 1,255 various editions of cookery books
from the late 19th century to the present, including Farmer,
Lincoln and modern writers; various modern texts. NV

The Library of Congress
Washington, D. C.

Within the vast holdings of the Library of Congress
are thousands of books relating to the culinary arts.   The
most easily distinguishable separate collection is that of the
more than 3,500 volumes of Katherine G. Bitting held in the
Rare Book and Special Collections Division.   The published
bibliography by Bitting is an incomplete reflection of the total
holdings, as it lists items not actually present within the
collection; further, the bibliography does not include many
items that are present.   There is a card index to the collection which is more complete.

Additionally, the Rare Book and Special Collections
Division holds a part of the collection of Elizabeth Pennell,
mostly 17th- and 18th-century French and English works.
A few of the authors represented are: Albert, Altamiras,
Apicius, Bruyerin, Carême, Dufour, Evelyn, Glasse, La
Varenne, Menon, Raffald, Randolph, Shirley, Viard, Woolley.
There is no guide to this collection other than a card index.
Other guides available in the Rare Book and Special Collec-
tions Division which can be used to locate culinary material
held by the Library of Congress include:

> Goff, Frederick. Incunabula in American Libraries,
> 1973. An annotated, working copy is available.
> (The Library of Congress is the largest repository
> of incunabula in the Western Hemisphere.)

> British Museum. Department of Printed Books.
> Short-title Catalogue of Books Printed in Italy and
> of Italian Books Printed in Other Countries from
> 1465 to 1600, 1958. A checked copy is maintained
> which indicates titles held by the Library of Con-
> gress.

> Marshall, Robert G.   Short-title Catalog of Books
> Printed in Italy ... 1501-1600, Held in Selected

North American Libraries, 1970.

Ricci, Seymour de. Census of Medieval and Renaissance Manuscripts in the United States and Canada,
1940. An annotated copy serves as a descriptive
guide and finding aid to the Library of Congress
collection.

The culinary holdings at the Library of Congress are
so scattered and so numerous that it is impossible to present
a proper survey within the limits of this study. A checklist
search would involve not only the use of the guides previously
mentioned, but also many other standard bibliographic guides,
unpublished listings held at the Library of Congress, as well
as the public catalog. There is an astounding wealth of
material here, spanning all centuries and all countries.

Appendix A

CULINARY BIBLIOGRAPHIES AND
BIBLIOGRAPHIC COMMENTARIES

Aebisher, Paul. "Un manuscritt valaisan du Viandier attribué
à Taillevent" in Vallesia, 1953, pp. 73-100.

Amerine, Maynard. A check list of books and pamphlets on
grapes and wine. Berkeley, University of California,
1951.

_____. A list of bibliographies and a selected list of pub-
lications that contain bibliographies on grapes, wines
and related subjects. Berkeley, University of California, 1971.

Aresty, Ester B. The delectable past. New York, Simon
and Schuster, 1964.

Axford, Lavonne Brady. English language cookbooks, 1600-
1973. Detroit, Gale Research Co., 1976.

Aylett, Mary. First catch your hare. London, MacDonald,
1965.

Baker, E. Allan. Bibliography of food. London, Butter-
worths, 1958.

Beck, Leonard. "A note on the librarian-author of the first
cookbook," in Quarterly Journal of the Library of
Congress, July 1975, pp. 238-253.

Birrell and Garnel. A catalogue from the collection of J.
E. Hodgkin and Dr. A. W. Oxford ... for sale, 1931.

Bitting, Katherine Golden. Gastronomic bibliography. San
Francisco, California, 1939.

Blake, John B. "The complete housewife," in Bulletin of

91

the History of Medicine, Vol. 49, No. 1, Spring 1975,
pp. 30-42.

Blum.   California Book Auction. Books of Marshall Blum.
San Francisco, California, 1973.

Blumenthal, Walter H.   "Potluck and peacock's tongues" in
Bookmen's Trio, Achille J. St. Onge, Worchester,
Massachusetts, 1961, pp. 53-86.

Book Auction Records. London, various dates.

Bootle, Valerie. A bibliography of hotel and catering opera-
tions. London, New University Education, 1970.

Brown, Eleanore. Culinary Americana. New York, Roving
Eye Press, 1961.

Cahoon, Herbert. Labels to accompany the Grolier Club exhibit held at the Pierpont Morgan Library. New York,
1960.

Carlson, Victoria. A bibliography for cookery investigation.
New York, Teachers College, Columbia University,
1927.

Cook, Margaret. America's charitable cooks. Kent, Ohio,
Margaret Cook, 1971.

_____. The cookery and gastronomy library of Mrs.
Thomas M. Scruggs and Margaret Cook. San Francisco, California Book Auction, Sept. 1977.

Cooper, Isabella. References ancient and modern to the
literature on beer and ale. New York, United Brewers
Industrial Foundation, 1937.

Cornell University. School of Hotel Administration Library.
A list of selected material from the Vehling Collection.
Ithaca, New York, n. d.

Crahan, Marcus. One hundred sixteen uncommon books on
food and drink. Berkeley, California, Bancroft Library, 1975.

Drexel, Theodore. Catalog der kochbücher sammlung.
Frankfurt, A. Osterrieth, 1885-1891.

DuRietz, Richard. Gastronomisk spegel; historisk översikt
    jamte for tekning över svenska kokoch hushalls böker
    framtill 1850. Stockholm, Thulins Antikvariat, 1953.

Ellwanger, George Herman. Pleasures of the table. New
    York, Doubleday, 1902. Bibliography, pp. 449-469.

Faccioli, Emilio. Arte della cucina; libri di ricette testi
    sopra lo scalo il trinciante ei vini dal. XIV al XIX
    se celo, Milano, Edizioni il Polifilo, 1966.

Ferguson, John. Bibliographical notes on histories of inventions
    and books of secrets. London, Holland Press, 1959.

Fleuret, Fernand. "Des livres de cuisine" in Arts et Métiers
    Graphiques, 1934.

Flower, Barbara. The Roman cookery book. London, Har-
    rap, 1958.

Furnivall, Frederick. Early English meals and manners.
    London, Trübner, 1868.

Georg, Karl. Verzeichnis der litterature über speise und
    trank. Hannover, Klindworth, 1888.

Glozer, Liselotte. California in the kitchen. Berkeley,
    David, 1960.

Goff, Frederick R. Incunabula in American libraries. New
    York, 1964.

Goff, Michael. Food and wine. London, National Book
    League, 1972.

Gourley, James E. "An annotated list of bibliographies of
    cookery books" in New York Public Library Bulletin,
    Vol. 41, 1937.

_____. "Regional American cookery, 1884-1934," in New
    York Public Library Bulletin, Vol. 39, 1935.

Gray, Sarah Virginia. A history of the publication of cook-
    books in the United States, 1796-1896. Chapel Hill,
    North Carolina, University of North Carolina, 1964.

Hackwood, Frederick. Good cheer. London, T. Fisher Un-
    win, 1911, Chapter XXI.

Handlist of cookery books and books about food in Guild Hall
       Library, London, nd.

Hazlitt, William. Old cookery books and ancient cuisine.
       London, Elliot Stock, 1902.

Herbert, A. Kenney. "The literature of cookery" in National
       Review, Vol. XXIV, Sept.-Feb., 1894-5. London,
       p. 675-684.

Institute of Masters of Wine. Library handlist, London, 1972.

Jeaffreson, John. A book about the table. London, Hurst
       and Blackett, 1875, Chapter XVII.

Kitchiner, William. The cooks oracle. London, Constable,
       1822. Bibliography pp. 24-27.

Lambert, M. Leon. Catalogue of the collection. England,
       Sotheby sale, 1966.

"Libros de cocina" in Bibliografia Hispanica, May 1949, pp.
       26-41.

Lincoln, Waldo. American cookery books, 1742-1860. Re-
       vised and enlarged by Eleanore Lowenstein. Massa-
       chusetts, American Antiquarian Society, 1929, 1954,
       1971.

Maggs Brothers, Ltd. Catalogue no. 645. Food and drink
       throughout the ages. London, Maggs Brothers, Ltd.
       1937.

Milham, Mary. "Apicius in the Northern Renaissance" in
       Bibliotheque d'Humanisme et Renaissance, 1970.

Murphy, Claudia Quigley. The fine collection of books formed
       by Mrs. Claudia Quigley Murphy. Anderson Galleries
       Catalog, no. 2063, New York, 1926.

Noling, A. W. Beverage literature. New Jersey, Scarecrow
       Press, 1971.

Norman, Barbara. Tales of the table. New Jersey, Pren-
       tice-Hall, 1972. Bibliography pp. 331-344.

Oxford, Arnold W. Collecting small things in a small way.

Notes from a collector's catalogue. "English books on cookery and carving up to ... 1699." London, J. & E. Bumpus, 1909.

_____. English cookery books to the year 1850. Oxford, U. P. London, 1913.

_____. Notes from a collector's catalog. London, Bumpus, 1909.

Pennell, Elizabeth. A guide for the greedy. Philadelphia, J. B. Lippincott, 1923. pp. vii-xxx.

_____. My cookery books. New York, Houghton Mifflin, 1903.

Pérez, Dionisio. Ruperto de Nola. Madrid, Pedro Sainz y Rodriguez, 1926.

Pichon, Jérôme. Catalogue de la bibliotheque de feu m le baron Jérôme Pichone. Sale in 3 parts 1897-98; catalogue des livres rares, 1869 sale; another sale in 1878.

_____. Le Viandier de Taillevent. Paris, Techever, 1892.

Priddat, R. E. Historical references on baking. Chicago, Illinois, American Institute of Baking, 1932.

Rhodes, D. E. "The Italian banquet, 1598 and its origins" in Italian Studies, 1972, pp. 60-63.

Rudolph, G. A. Receipt book and household manual. Manhattan, Kansas, Kansas State University Library, 1968.

Schraemli, Harry. Catalogue of a collection of books and manuscripts of the 15th to 20th century on food and wine from the well-known library of Harry Schraemli. London, Sotheby and Company, February, 1971.

Catalogue de la vente. (Iere vente) 1971; (IIe vente) 1972.

_____. A résumé of the great Herr Schraemli collection. Beverly Hills, Harry A. Levinson, 1963.

_____. Zweitausend jahre gastronomische literatur. Zürich, 1942.

Shircliffe. Parke-Bernet Galleries, Inc. Books on cookery
    XV-XX (centuries) collected by ... Arnold Shircliffe.
    Parke-Bernet Galleries, Inc. , New York, 1954.

Short-title catalogue of books printed in England,
    Scotland and Ireland, 1475-1640 (Pollard & Redgrave)
    London, 1956.

Short-title catalogue of books printed in England 1641-
    1700 (Wing), New York, 1951.

Short-title catalogue of books printed in German speak-
    ing countries 1455 to 1600, London, 1962.

Short-title catalogue of books printed in Italy 1465 to
    1600, London, 1958.

Short-title catalogue of books printed in the Nether-
    lands and Belgium, 1470 to 1600, London, 1965.

Simmons, Amelia. American cookery (a facsimilie). New
    York, Oxford U. P. , 1958, Introduction pp. i-xxiv.

Simon, André. Bibliotheca bacchia. London, Holland Press,
    1927. (Reprint 1972).

_____ . Bibliotheca gastronomica. London, Wine and
    Food Society, 1952.

_____ . Bibliotheca vinaria. London, G. Richards, 1913.

_____ . An exhibition of rare printed books assembled
    and annotated by André Simon. London National Book
    League, 1961.

_____ . Food. London, Burke Publishing Co. , 1949.
    Chapter IV.

Stark, Lewis M. The Whitney cookery collection. New
    York, New York Public Library, 1959.

"Survey of the world's food literature [an exhibition of the
    collection of Joseph D. Vehling]" in Hotel Bulletin
    and the Nations Chefs, 1931.

Swinton, Cordelia W. A bibliography of the cookbooks and
    gastronomical treatises in the Pennsylvania State Uni-
    versity collection. University Park, Pennsylvania
    State University, 1972.

Taylor, Clara Mae. <u>Annotated international bibliography of nutrition education.</u> New York, Teachers College, Columbia University, 1971.

Thudicum, John. <u>The spirt of cookery.</u> London, Bailliere, Tindall and Cos, 1875. Chapter II.

Uhler, John E. <u>The Rochester Clarke bibliography of Louisiana cookery.</u> Iberville Parish Library, Plaquemine, Louisiana, 1966.

U. S. Dept. of Agriculture. <u>Food and nutrition information and educational materials center catalog.</u> Washington, D. C. , U. S. Dept. of Agriculture, 1973 to date.

Vanossi, Lorenzo. <u>Bibliografia gastronomica italiana fin al 1950.</u> Pinerolo, Editrice Technica Molitoria, 1964.

Vara, Albert. <u>Food and beverage industries: a bibliography and guidebook.</u> Detroit, Gale, 1970.

Vehling, Joseph. <u>A catalogue of ... gastrosophical and magiric documents dating from the 15th to the ... 19th century.</u> Chicago, 1927.

_____. "Martino and Platina, exponents of Renaissance cookery" in <u>Hotel Bulletin and the Nation's Chefs,</u> 1932.

Vicaire, Georges. <u>Bibliographie gastronomique.</u> Paris, P. Rouquette et Fils, 1890.

Vinceus, S. <u>An evaluation of the Vehling collection ...</u> Ithaca, New York, Cornell University, School of Hotel Administration, nd.

Vintner's Company. <u>Loan exhibition of drinking vessels, books and documents, etc. , held at Vintner's Hall.</u> London, June-July 1933.

Warner, R. <u>Antiquitates culinariae.</u> London, 1791.

Westbury. <u>Catalog of the Westbury collection.</u> London, Sotheby & Co. , 1965.

_____. <u>Handlist of Italian cookery books.</u> Florence, Leo S. Olschki, 1963.

Willan, Anne. Great cooks and their recipes. N.Y., Mc-
     Graw Hill, 1977.

Wiswe, Hans. Kulturgeschichte der kochkunst. Munich,
     H. Moos, 1970.

Yost, Genevieve. "The compleat housewife ... a bibliograph-
     ical study." William and Mary Quarterly, October
     1938.

Appendix B

SECONDARY HISTORICAL TEXTS AND REFERENCES

Aaron, Jean-Paul. Le mangeur de XIXe siecle. Paris, Robert Laffont, 1973.

_____. The art of eating in France. London, Peter Owen, 1975.

Académie des Gastonomes. Dictionnaire de l'académie. Paris, 1962.

Ainsworth-Davis, J. R. Cooking through the centuries. New York, Dutton, 1931.

Alberini, Massimo. Storia del pranzo all'italiana, Milan, Rizzoli, 1966.

Allen, Herbert Warner. A history of wine. London, Saber, 1961.

American Heritage. American heritage cookbook and illustrated history of American eating and drinking. New York, Simon and Schuster, 1964.

Andrews, Julia. Breakfast, dinner and tea. N.Y., Appleton, 1859.

Andrieu, Pierre. Fine bouche. London, Cassell and Company, 1956.

_____. Histoire du restaurant en France. Paris, La Journee Vinicole, 1955.

Arnold, John. Origin and history of beer and brewing ... Chicago, Wahl-Henius Institute, 1911.

Athenaeus. Deipnosophists. Various editions.

99

Aylett, Mary. First catch your hare. London, Mcdonald,
    1965.

Barber, Richard. Cooking from Rome to the Renaissance.
    London, Allen Lane, 1973.

Barrows, Anna. An outline on the history of cookery. New
    York, Teachers College, 1915.

Barry, Edward. Observations, historical, critical and medi-
    cal on the wines of the ancients. London, T. Cadell,
    1775.

Baudet, Florence. De maaltije en de keuken in de middeleu-
    wen. Leiden, A. W. Sijthoff, 1904.

Bauer, Hans. Tisch und tafel in alten zeiten. Leipsig,
    Koehler und Amelang, 1967.

Beeuwkes, Adelia. Essays on the history of nutrition and
    dietetics. Chicago, American Dietetic Association,
    1967.

Bemelmans, Ludwig. La bonne table. New York, Simon
    and Schuster, 1964.

Berkhout, Barbara. "Taillevent" in Gourmet, February 1968.

Bickerdyke, John. Curiosities of ale and beer. London,
    Spring Books, 1889.

Blond, Georges. Histoire pittoresque de notre alementation.
    Paris, Librarie Arthelme Fayard, 1960.

Bodet, R. Toques blanches et habits noires. Paris, Dorbon,
    1939.

Booth, Sally. Hung, strung, and potted. New York, Crown,
    1971.

Bourgeat, Jacques. Le plaisirs de la table en France.
    Paris, Hachette, 1963.

Brett, Gerard. Dinner is served. Connecticut, Archon, 1968.

Briffaut, Eugene. Paris à table. Paris, Hertzel, 1846.

Broadhurst, Jean. "What our Colonial ancestors ate as told

by Samuel Pepys 1660-1669" in Western Dietition, Sept. 1926.

Brothwell, Don R. Food in antiquity. New York, Praeger, 1969.

Bruyerinus, Johannus. De re cibaria. Various editions.

Burnet, Regula. Ann Cook and friend. London, Oxford Univ. Press, 1936.

Burnett, John. Plenty and want. London, Thomas Nelson, 1966.

Butler, F. Wine and winelands of the world. London, Fisher Unwin, 1926.

Cannon, Poppy. Eating European. New York, Award, 1968.

Carson, Jane. Colonial Virginia cookery. Charlottesville, University Press of Virginia, 1965.

Castelot, Andre. L'Histoire à table. Paris, Plon, 1972.

Chakravarty, Indria. Saga of Indian food. New Delhi, Sterling, 1972.

Chang, K. C. "Food and food vessels in ancient China" in Transactions of the New York Academy of Sciences, June, 1973.

_____. Food in Chinese culture. New Haven, Yale Univ. Press, 1977.

Chatillon-Plessis. La vie à table a la fin du XIXe siecle. Paris, Didot, 1894.

Child, Theodore. Delicate feasting. New York, Harper and Bros., 1890.

Ciacconius, Petrus. De trinclinio Romano. Various editions.

Clair, Colin. Kitchen and table. 1964.

Cooper, Charles. The English table in history and literature. London, Low, 1929.

Cosman, Madeline. Fabulous feasts. N.Y., Braziller, 1976.

Craig, Elizabeth. Court favourites. London, Andre Deutsch,
    1953.

Cummings, Robert O. The American and his food. New
    York, Arno Press, 1941.

Current biography. Various editions.

Darby, William. The gift of Osiris. N.Y. , Academic Press,
    1977.

DeSalis, Harriet Anne. The history of cookery. London,
    Hutchinson and Co. , 1898.

DesOmbiaux, Maurice. L'art de manger et son histoire.
    Paris, Payot, 1928.

DeVillefosse, René-Heron. Histoire et géographie gourmandes
    de Paris. Paris, Payot, 1928.

Dictionnaire de l'academie des gastronomes. Paris, Prisma,
    1962.

Dion, Roger. Histoire de la vigne. Paris, 1959.

Donovan, Maria. "The entertaining Isabella d'este" in Gour-
    met, June, 1971, pp. 44+.

Doran, John. Table traits with something on them. New
    York, Redfield, 1855.

Drummond, J. C. The Englishman's food. London, Readers
    Onion, 1959.

Dumay, Raymond. De la gastronomie Francaise. Paris,
    Stock, 1969.

DuPaillon, Robert. Le coupe de fourchette. Ostede, Editions
    Erel, 1963.

Du Rietz, Richard. Gastronomisk spegel; historisk översikt
    jamte fortekning over svenska kok-och hushalls-bocker
    fram till 1850. Stockholm, 1953.

Ellwanger, George H. Pleasures of the table. New York,
    Doubleday, 1902.

Emerson, Edward. The story of the vine. New York, Put-
    nam, 1901.

Encyclopaedia Britannica Macropedia.   Article on gastronomy,
      1974.

Faccioli, Emilo.   Arte della cucina; libri di ricette testi
      sopra lo scalo il trinciante e i vini dal XIV al XIX
      secolo, Milano, Edizioni il Pulifilo, 1966.

Farber, Seymour M.   Food and civilization.   Springfield,
      Illinois, Charles C. Thomas, 1966.

Favre, Joseph.   Dictionnaire universel de cuisine et d'hygiene
      alimentaire.   Paris, Chez Tous Les Lib. 1891.

Fisher, Mary.   Serve it forth.   New York, World Book Co. ,
      1937.

Fitzgibbon, Theodora.   The food of the Western world.   New
      York, Quadrangle, 1976.

Francisque, Michel and Fournier, M.   Histoire des hotelleries
      Paris, Delahaye, 1859.

Franklin, Alfred.   La vie privée d'autrefois.   Vol. III, La
      cuisine.   Vol. VI, Les repas, Paris, E. Plon, 1881-
      1902.

Fuller, John.   Chef's manual of kitchen management.   London,
      Batsford, 1962.

Furnas, C. C.   The story of man and his food.   New York,
      New Home Library, 1937.

Garlin, Gustave.   Cuisine ancienne.   Paris, Garnier Frères,
      1894.

Gault, Henri.   Guide gourmand de la France.   Paris, Li-
      brairie Hachette, 1970.

Gerard, Charles.   L'ancienne Alsace à table.   Colmar, 1862.

Gottschalk, Alfred.   Histoire de l'alimentation et de la gas-
      tronomie.   Paris, Editions Hippocrate, 1948.

Graubard, Mark.   Man's food, its rhyme or reason.   New
      York, Macmillan, 1943.

Grimley, Gordon.   The Victorian cookery book.   London,
      Abelard-Schuman, 1973.

Grounds-Peace, Zara. Mrs. Grounds-Peace's old cookery
    notebook. London, International Wine and Food So-
    ciety, 1971.

Guégan, Bertrand. Le cuisinier Français. France, Emile-
    Paul Frères, 1934.

_____. La fleur de la cuisine Français. Paris, Sirene,
    1920.

Guerrin, Olindo. La tavola el cucina nei secoli XIV e XV
    conferenza tenuta all' exposizione di Torino, it 21
    giugno, 1884. Firenze, G. Barbera, 1884.

Guy, Christian. Illustrated history of French cuisine. New
    York, Orion Press, 1962.

Hachez, Henri. La cuisine à travers l'histoire. 1900.

Hackwood. Good cheer. New York, Strugis and Walton,
    1911.

Hale. Horizon cookbook and illustrated history of eating and
    drinking through the ages. New York, Doubleday,
    1968.

Hampson, John. The English at table. London, Collins,
    1946.

Harrison, Molly. The kitchen in history. New York, Scrib-
    ners, 1972.

Hartley, Dorothy. Food in England. London, McDonald,
    1954.

Hayward, Abraham. The art of dining. N.Y., Putnam, 1899.

Hazlitt, W. Carew. Old cookery books and ancient cuisine.
    London, Elliot Stock, 1886.

Henderson, Alexander. History of ancient and modern wines.
    1824.

Herbodeau, Eugène. George Auguste Escoffier. London,
    Practical Press, 1955.

Hillard, Sam. Hog meat and hoecake. Illinois, Southern
    Illinois University Press, 1972.

Hyams, Edward. <u>Dionysus</u>. New York, Macmillan, 1965.

Hyde, H. Montgomery. <u>Mr. and Mrs. Beeton</u>. London, Harrap, 1951.

Jacobs, Jay. <u>Gastronomy</u>. N.Y., Newsweek Books, 1975.

James, Margery. <u>Studies in the medieval wine trade</u>. Oxford, Clarendon, 1971.

Jeaffreson, John Cordy. <u>A book about table</u>. London, Hurst & Blackett, 1875.

Johnson, Lois S. <u>What we eat</u>. Chicago, Rand McNally, 1969.

Jones, Evan. <u>American food</u>. New York, Dutton, 1975.

Kudriaffsky, Eufemia. <u>Die historiche küche</u>. Weir, U. Hartlebens Verlag, 1880.

Lacroix, Paul. <u>Histoire de l'imprimerie et des arts et professions</u>.

Lamb, Richard. <u>In celebration of wine and life</u>. New York, Drake, 1974.

Lamprey, Louise. <u>The story of cookery</u>. New York, A. Stokes, 1940.

Lawall, Charles. "The romance of cookery" in <u>Popular Science Talks</u>, 1928.

Lawton, Mary. <u>The Queen of cooks and some kings</u>. New York, Boni and Liveright, 1924.

Layard, A. H. "Renaissance cookery" in <u>Murray's Magazine</u>, Vol. IX, January-June 1891, London, pp. 326-345.

Lebault, Armand. <u>La table et le repas à travers les siecles</u>. Paris, Lucien Laveur, 1910.

LeGrand d'Aussy, Pierre. <u>Histoire de la vie privée des Francois</u>. Paris, Laurent-Beaupré, 1782.

Lewicki, Tadeuse. <u>West African food in the Middle Ages</u>. London, Cambridge University Press, 1974.

Lillywhite, Bryant. London coffee houses. London, Allen
    and Unwin, 1963.

Linsenmeyer, Helen Walker. From fingers to finger bowls.
    San Diego Union-Tribune, 1972.

Lorwin, Madge. Dining with William Shakespeare. New
    York, Atheneum, 1976.

Lowenberg, Marian. Food and man. New York, John Wiley,
    1968.

McKendry, Maxine. Seven centuries of English cooking.
    London, Weidenfeld & Nicholson, 1973.

McNeill, F. Marian. The Scot's kitchen. London, Blackie,
    1963.

Manchester, Herbert. The evolution of cooking and heating.
    Fuller and Warren, 1917.

Martin, Charles. Foods and culinary utensils of the ancients.
    N.Y., Canter, 1906.

Martyn, Charles. Food and culinary utensils of the ancients.
    1906.

Masters, Anthony. Rosa Lewis. London, Weidenfeld and
    Nicolson, 1977.

MD, Medical News, "Chef extraordinaire," Article on Soyer,
    July, 1973.

_____, "Existential epicure," Article on MFK Fisher, Feb.
    1972.

_____. Series of articles on banquets, 1972-1973.

Mead, William Edward. The English medieval feast. Lon-
    don, 1931.

Melikan, K. Cyrus. Wonder of food. New York, Appleton,
    1961.

Mestayer de Enchagüe, Maria. Historia de la gastronomia.
    Madrid, Espasa-Calpa, 1943.

Michel, Francisque. Histoire des hotellerie caberets ...
    Paris, 1851.

Moffatt, Donald. "Grimod de la Reynière" in Gourmet, January, 19??.

Montagné, Prosper. Larousse gastronomique. New York, Crown, 1961.

_____. New Larousse gastronomique, N. Y., Crown, 1977.

Morel, Julian. The caterer's companion. London, Pitman, 1973.

Morris, Helen. Portrait of a chef. Cambridge, Cambridge Univ. Press, 1938.

Moss, Peter. Meals through the ages. London, Harrap, 1958.

New York City. Metropolitan Museum of Art. The secular spirit. New York, Dutton, 1975.

Newhall, Beaumont. "Sugar architecture of the great chef Carême" in Vogue, n. d.

Nicolardot, Louis. Histoire de la table. Paris, E. Dentu, 1868.

Norman, Barbara. Tales of the table. New York, Prentice-Hall, 1972.

O'leary, Brian. "From the tables of Kings." Series of articles in Cooking for Profit, 1967-1968.

Oliver, Raymond. Gastronomy of France. Ohio, World Publishing Co. , 1967.

Page, Edward. The Master chefs. London, Edward Arnold, 1971.

Palmer, Arnold. Movable feasts. London, Oxford University Press, 1952.

Perl, Lila. Foods and festivals of the Danube lands. Cleveland, World, 1969.

_____. Red flannel hash and shoo-fly pie. Cleveland, World, 1965.

_____. Rice, spice and bitter oranges. Cleveland, World, 1967.

Prakash, Om.   Food and drink in ancient India.   New Delhi,
    Mushi Ram Manohar Lal, 1961.

Pullar, Philippa.   Consuming passions.   Boston, Little Brown,
    1970.

Pyke, Magnus.   Food and society.   London, John Murray,
    1968.

_____ .   Man and food.   New York, McGraw Hill.

Redmayne, Paul.   Britain's food.   London, John Murray,
    1963.

Root, Waverly.   "Early American cookery" in Gourmet,   Feb.
    1976.

_____ .   Eating in America.   N.Y. , Morrow, 1976.

_____ .   The food of France.   New York, Knopf, 1958.

_____ .   The food of Italy.   New York, Atheneum, 1971.

Royal cookbook.   Parents Magazine Press, 1971.

Sailland, M. E.   Les fines gueules de France: Gastonomes,
    Gourmets.   Paris, Didot, 1935.

Sass, Lorna.   To the king's taste.   N.Y. , Metropolitan Mu-
    seum of Art, 1975.

_____ .   To the queen's taste.   N.Y. , Metropolitan Museum
    of Art, 1976.

_____ .   Dinner with Tom Jones.   N.Y. , Metropolitan Mu-
    seum of Art, 1977.

Schiedlausky, Gunther.   Essen und trinken.   Munich, Prestel,
    1959.

Schraemli, Harry.   Von Lucullus zu Escoffier.   Zurich,
    Interverlag, 1949.

Seltman, Charles.   Wine in the ancient world.   1957.

Simmons, Amelia.   American cookery (a facsimile).   1958.
    New York, Oxford U. P. , introduction pp. i-xxiv.

Simon, André.   Drink.   London, Burke Publishing Co. , 1948.

_____. Food. London, Burke Publishing Co., 1949.

_____. The Star Chamber dinner accounts. London, Wine and Food Society, 1959.

Smallzried, Kathleen. Everlasting pleasure. New York, Appleton-Century-Crofts, 1956.

Smith, Henry. Classical recipes of the world. New York, Macmillan, 1955.

Smith, Margaret. Epicures companion. New York, David McKay, 1962.

Soyer, Alexis. Pantropheon. London, Tichnor, Reed and Fields, 1853.

Spain, Nancy. Mrs. Beeton and her husband. London, Collins, 1948.

Specht, Franz Anton. Gastmahler und trinkgelage beiden deutscher ... bis in neunte Jahrhundert. Stuttgart, 1887.

Stewart, Katie. Cooking and eating. London, Hart-Davis, MacGibbon, 1975.

Street, Julian. Table topics. New York, Knopf, 1959.

La table (periodical), 1868.

Tannahill, Reay. The fine art of food. New York, A. S. Barnes, 1970.

_____. Food in history. New York, Stein and Day, 1973.

Thomas, Gertrude. Foods of our forefathers. Philadelphia, F. A. Davis Co., 1941.

Thudicum, J. L. W. The spirit of cookery. London, Baillière, Tindall and Cox, 1895.

Time-Life. Foods of the world. A series of volumes by various authors.

Trager, James. ... Food book. New York, Grossman, 1970.

110   Secondary References

Vehling, Joseph. Platina and the rebirth of man. Chicago, Walter Hill, 1941.

Verdot, C. Historiographie de la table. Paris, Delaunay, 1833.

Verrill, A. Hyatt. Foods America gave the world. Boston, Page, 1937.

Warner, Richard. Antiquitates culinariae. London, R. Blamire, 1791.

Wason, Betty. Cooks, gluttons, and gourmets. New York, Doubleday, 1962.

Wechsberg, Joseph. "Gastrongmy" in Quality, edited by Louis Kronenberger. N.Y., Atheneum, 1969.

Whitehill, Jane. Food, drink and recipes of early New England. Mass., Old Sturbridge Village, 1963.

Willan, Anne. Great cooks and their recipes. N.Y., McGraw-Hill, 1977.

Wilson, Anne. Food and drink in Britain. London, Constable, 1973.

Wiswe, Hans. Kulturgeschichte der kochkunst. Munich, H. Mous, 1970.

Wright, Lawrence. Home fires burning. London, Routledge & Kegan, 1964.

Wühr, Hans. Alte Kucher und Küchen geräte. Darmstadt, F. Schneekluter, 1955.

Younger, William. Gods, men and wine. London, Wine and Food Society, 1966.

INDEX